THE
MENTORING
ADVANTAGE

CREATING THE NEXT
GENERATION OF LEADERS

FLORENCE STONE

Dearborn™
Trade Publishing
A **Kaplan Professional** Company

Vice President and Publisher: Cynthia A. Zigmund
Acquisitions Editor: Jonathan Malysiak
Senior Project Editor: Trey Thoelcke
Interior Design: Lucy Jenkins
Cover Design: Design Solutions
Typesetting: the dotted i

© 2004 by Florence Stone

Published by Dearborn Trade Publishing
A Kaplan Professional Company

Printed in the United States of America

04   05   06   10   9   8   7   6   5   4   3   2   1

Library of Congress Cataloging-in-Publication Data

Stone, Florence M.
    The mentoring advantage : creating the next generation of leaders / Florence Stone.
        p.   cm.
    Includes index.
    ISBN 0-7931-8692-7
    1. Mentoring in business.   2. Employees—Training of.   3. Career development.   I. Title.
    HF5385.S77 2004
    658.3'124—dc22

                                                                      2004012766

C o n t e n t s

PART FOUR
THE HOW-TO OF FACILITATED PROGRAMS

*T**he Mentoring Advantage* is a welcome addition to the library of leaders. Florence Stone's book comes at the height of interest in mentoring in all sectors—public, private, and government. It addresses questions that organizations and executives, managers, and others have as they consider either becoming a mentor or initiating a formal mentoring program.

I myself have been a mentor on several occasions—while the head of the Girl Scouts and as president and chief executive officer, and now chairman, of the Leader to Leader Institute, formerly the Drucker Foundation.

Let me share with you a story related to my experience as a mentor.

Several years ago, I was at a prestigious university where I had been invited to speak. I would be speaking both at noon and later in the evening. While there, I was invited to join a small group of faculty members, all women, in an informal dialogue. I was delighted to join them that afternoon, for that experience gave me a new understanding of a critical factor—an essential support—in the leadership development of men and women in the university world, as well as in business, nonprofit, and government sectors.

The issue these accomplished, tenured, published professors wanted to discuss was the retention of younger faculty members: young women, 28 to 30 years of age. Unfortunately, too often, these young women joined the faculty only to leave a few years later. The big question the group wanted me to discuss with it was: "What can we do to retain these valuable young faculty members?"

I responded with a question of my own: "How many of you are mentoring these young women?" I was greeted with silence. Not one faculty member had been a mentor to one of these valuable young women that the group said it wanted to keep on the faculty.

My response was simple: "Until every person in this room is mentoring a young faculty member, we cannot complain when they leave all too soon."

They responded in term: "How many young women do you mentor?" I replied, "three," and then described the three young women I have been mentoring for several years.

I talked about LCR Carla Grantham, U.S. Coast Guard. She had called on me to discuss a substantial fellowship she had just received and wanted to use it at the then Drucker Foundation for six months. It would enable her to live in New York, shadow me, travel with me, attend meetings where I was speaking, and work in my office for six months. As attractive as this opportunity was, I felt it would not be fair to have her spend so much of her valuable six months of study in airports, as I travel at least twice a week speaking in this country or abroad. I suggested, instead, that she find another place to apply her fellowship. Instead, I would be her mentor. We could meet every few months in New York or Washington, and she could shadow me at our conferences, or other events. Acting as her mentor would be the best way I could help her with her leadership growth.

It has been six years, and today Lt. Commander Grantham is at a remarkable point in her career. She recently received her graduate degree in communication and is serving as the officer responsible for the recruitment of Naval and Coast Guard officers, inspiring young students and fellow service members with her example.

In these six years, I have discovered that mentoring is circular, and that I've learned more from LCR Carla Grantham than she has learned from me.

Then I told the faculty members at that university about the second young woman I mentor, a student from Senzhen, China. I met Lin Yuang and her mother when I was speaking to a group of Chinese business leaders in Senzhen. After the speech, the mother and Lin Yuang came up to me and said they felt I should be the daughter's mentor. I said I would be honored, and with e-mail, we could have remarkable exchanges. I did not hear from my new mentee for months, then one day she called, said she was enrolled at the State University on Staten Island in New York, and was ready to begin our mentoring sessions. And so we did. We have been on an adventure in cross-cultural mentoring ever since. When Lin and I have our scheduled luncheons together, both of us learn when she looks at her list and says, "Now in your culture, what does this means when someone says, etc. etc." Our dialogue brightens my day.

When Lin Yuang's parents visited her last Labor Day, the three came to spend the holiday at my house in Easton, Pennsylvania, and taught me to make Chinese dumplings, while I introduced them to Cornish pasties.

Commander Grantham is of African-American descent, Lin Yuang is Chinese, and the third mentee is white, a successful young lawyer, and a business leader.

Each of my mentees has great depth, great potential, and great present performance. Because we are not all white, there is an enormously rich dimension in the diversity of my small mentoring group.

I shared these stories with the faculty members, and they listened with great interest, because I was not sharing theory—these were living case studies about the lives of four women—three young, the fourth older, but each finding many of the values and benefits Florence Stone writes about in her book *The Mentoring Advantage.*

In mentoring of young school children by older students, students bring a new excitement to the classrooms as well as to their lives. Because mentoring is coming into its own at every level in every sector, particularly in public and private schools, we see a new generation emerging with leadership potential, leadership experience enhanced by the mentoring experience.

As I look at the three young women I mentor, they represent all three sectors: corporate, government, and academic. What is interesting to me, in all of the mentoring experiences I have had, is that the other person initiated it, we agreed upon the ways we would work, how, when, and why. The *why* was the most important part of the agreement, and always learning and growing were a part of the expectations. In the past, many of us have entered into these mentoring relationships without the clarity, the understanding of roles, responsibilities/expectations, the means by which we would measure results, or definitions of all the roles the mentor would play.

This is especially what makes Florence Stone's definitive study of mentoring so valuable. In a very readable manner, she also explains how organizations can go about developing formal programs, from setting program goals to development of the agreement between the mentor and mentee to management of the mentoring process, and it is a process. But this book isn't only for those organizations that want to formalize mentoring. It is for each and every individual, regardless of position or sector of society, young or old, who want guidance as they embark upon this adventure in human relationships.

Our tenuous times increase the interest of both those who wish to be mentored and those who would mentor. The value of the experience to both is enhanced when the mentoring is circular. There are many books on coaching or counseling, or mentoring. Someone has said that coaching is "somewhere between the couch and the confessional."

This book defines the differences, describes the systems, and provides guidelines for development and measurements for results.

In the end mentoring is all about relationships, all about human growth and potential, all about skills and the spirit within.

Mentoring requires leadership, and courage, on the part of the mentee to engage in this new relationship, and the same for the mentor who must be willing to open up his or her life. It takes courage to be mentored and still more to mentor, and for both a commitment to partner in an adventure in personal leadership learning and growing.

Mentoring has a proud, historical background. In the Spring 2004 issue of *MWorld*, there is even mention of a lesson on mentoring from the Lewis and Clark Expedition: "Seek out mentors to expand your horizon. Thomas Jefferson helped Lewis understand that the mission was not just about commerce; it was about nation building. And George Rogers Clark, a Revolutionary War hero, similarly influenced his younger brother's decision to join the expedition for the future of America." Vision of the future, expanding horizons, coming through two great leaders of our country's past with a powerful message for leaders of the future.

Florence Stone leads the way in *The Mentoring Advantage.*

Frances Hesselbein
Chairman of the Board
Leader to Leader Institute

WHAT MENTORING IS ALL ABOUT— AND WHAT IT ISN'T ABOUT

Mentoring is a trend sweeping through corporate America—and with cause. In interviews, almost all leaders today have pointed to one or more individuals who had a major influence on their professional lives, if not both their professional *and* personal lives. Being mentored has come to be considered one of the great things we can all do to advance our careers. So, today, hundreds of thousands of informal relationships are occurring as ambitious employees and managers—not to mention would-be entrepreneurs—look for ways to achieve their career goals faster with the help of a more experienced advisor or counselor. Structured or facilitated company programs are also on an increase as organizations see that mentoring programs can shorten learning tracks, speed up managerial advancement, and build the next generation of leaders.

WHAT'S IN IT FOR ME?

Those who are mentored report that mentoring relationships raise their morale, increase their capabilities, and contribute to shared listening. But the benefits are not one-sided. Mentors have found that the experience can benefit them as much as it helps the mentees. Those who act as mentors grow their coaching and counseling skills, expand their access to information and build contacts, and gain a sense of well-being from sharing their know-how with another. Mentors tell me that they have become better listeners, demonstrate greater interest in coaching staff, and find it improves overall communication. So, it can be a very satisfying and beneficial partnership.

If you are considering becoming a mentor, which is probably why you picked up this book, you should have a clear understanding of the role and responsibilities—and the value you can get and give as a mentor. But, first, I should clarify what mentoring is. Despite the popularity of mentoring, misconceptions still abound about the relationship.

UNMUDDYING THE WATERS

For instance, many articles about mentoring mistakenly describe situations in which a person has been influenced by another. The person had an influence on someone but never realized that he was regarded as someone to emulate. As such, he was a role model for the person. Because the individual never knew that the other person aspired to be like him, and did nothing to help the individual achieve the goal, he never was the individual's mentor.

Likewise, an influential person may affect the career of another by recommending that person for promotion or for a plum assignment that opens up. In this instance, the person who made an impact on the other person's career might have known the person, but the beneficiary of the recommendation might never have known about the part the person played in her career. In recommending the individual, the person may have been an advocate or sponsor, bringing the individual to the attention of the person who would make the final decision. But, while impacting the person's life, the influential individual was not her mentor. In a mentoring relationship, the mentor and the mentee enter into an agreement—a written document in most structured programs or a verbal discussion in informal relationships—to interact in ways to facilitate the learning, growth, and skill development of either or both of them.

Mentoring and coaching are also confused. By definition, coaching is about one-on-one instruction. In practice, it is a means of providing feedback to sustain and improve performance. Coaching is often confused with mentoring because coaching is a critical element of mentoring. Mentoring, however, is a process by which a wise and helpful guide or advisor uses experience to show a person how to avoid mistakes he or she made earlier in his career or otherwise help advance the individual in her career. The original perception of a mentor was as a protector, which explains the use of the medieval term *protégé*—literally, the "protected one"—to describe the mentee.

Note that I did not suggest a mentor needs to be older than the mentee or protégé. This is another misconception. Someone is a mentor because that person has knowledge or experience to bring to the relationship from which the other party can benefit. In an ideal relationship, the learning process goes both ways. The mentee also has knowledge and experience that are valued by the mentor and willingly shares them with the more experienced person.

While the mentor may serve as a role model for the mentee—or broker, sponsor, or even cheerleader—the relationship is overt and has some specific outcomes in mind. The relationship can exist for a few months or extend over years. The friendship that is the product of the mentoring relationship can last the parties' lives. As mentor and mentee, the two individuals meet at various times, best agreed-on early in the relationship to ensure that the contact is ongoing, because mentoring isn't a single event but very much a process.

WHO WAS THE FIRST MENTOR?

Some of the confusion surrounding mentoring stems from its roots which can be traced as far back as the Stone Age when older members of a tribe or a clan taught youngsters how to hunt, gather, prepare food, and fight off enemies. Selected younger members were trained by talented cave artists, shamans, and healers to ensure that those skills were perpetuated.

We first see an account of mentoring in the book of Proverbs in the Old Testament, which, according to scholars, dates from the tenth century B.C. However, the first use of the term is found in Homer's *The Odyssey*. The mythical figure, Mentor, was undoubtedly drawn from the real life of his time. Often, an older man served as advisor to a younger man. Indeed, *mentoring*—from the Greek word meaning to counsel—is defined as a sustained relationship between a youth and an adult. Through continued involvement, the adult offers support, guidance, and assistance as the younger person goes through a difficult period, faces new challenges, or works to solve problems.

In *The Odyssey*, Odysseus, king of Ithaca, goes to fight in the Trojan War and entrusts the care of his household and the training of his son, Telemachus, to a servant named Mentor. For ten years, Mentor taught Telemachus not solely how to rule but also the values he would need as a man. Odysseus wandered vainly for ten years in an effort to return home.

Throughout history, there have always been individuals, scattered through all societies, who invested personal time to help others achieve more than they

(handwritten marginal note: What happened to the Proverb examples here?)

would have without that assistance. Some of these relationships have gone down in history, like Socrates and Plato, Haydn and Beethoven, and Freud and Jung. The fathers of western philosophy regarded the transmission of experience as nothing more than a moral duty. Socrates declared that knowledge is the most valuable thing a person can have and that it must be shared for the good of the community.

———— Versions of mentoring relationships can be found not only in ancient Greece but throughout the ages. By the Middle Ages, a system had developed whereby apprentices learned their trades under masters who had gone through the same process themselves. Sometimes, the masters were related to their apprentices, but more often they were not relatives but skilled artisans who shared their skills with youths in return for near-free labor. For centuries, an apprenticeship was virtually the only method by which advanced technical skills and knowledge were shared.

Apprenticeships were not limited to manual labor. Mentoring occurred also in religious orders. Medicine, law, and politics were all taught in the same way—an experienced practitioner taught his junior.

This model hasn't really changed today. Apprenticeships have only been replaced with vocational training. Medical interns and law students are expected to work for a certain period of time under a senior practitioner before they are considered fully qualified. In universities, senior professors play the classic mentor's role with graduate students, sharing their knowledge and judgments to help in the completion of master's and doctorate papers. And we can't forget the mentoring role played by members of the clergy, social workers, and concerned volunteers who act as mentors to help people to cope with a variety of personal problems.

In organizations, we see two versions of mentoring. Just as in the far away past informal mentoring occurred in any community, so it continues to occur in almost every organization. After all, firms have their own cultures, their own leadership, their own body politic. Within businesses, mentors can teach mentees or protégés the "unwritten rules of the organization" as well as skills, abilities, and knowledge they gained bit by bit, day by day.

MENTORING BEFORE THE NEW MILLENIUM

Until the end of the twentieth century, in most organizations, mentoring was done informally, especially when both mentor and protégé were in white-collar positions. Senior executives would "adopt" talented managers or up-and-coming employees. The nature of the mentoring had several key characteristics.

- *A single-minded focus on career advancement.* After all, the goal of the mentees was to speed their professional advancement.
- *A belief that the mentor would be a protector.* The mentor was seen as an advocate of the less experienced person, using his or her network to support the mentee's upward progress.
- *A desire to clone look-alike, think-alike, act-alike managers.* The mentors sought out those whose aspirations resembled their own at that age, as well as their backgrounds, genders, and cultures. So, too often, male executives mentored male managers. Women still had a glass ceiling to break through and an old boys' network to fight.
- *A vision of mentoring that was fundamentally elitist.* Mentoring wasn't designed to speed development of all managers. Rather, it was a means to assimilate high-potential males into the inner management circle.
- *Little concern about corporate mission or strategy.* The emphasis was on the mentee's career development, not the development of the organization.
- *Indifference to hidden talent.* The focus was on what prospective mentees did, not their potential, so many young people who could have profited from mentoring were ignored, despite their career aspirations.

In some organizations, this limited approach to mentoring continues. But at the end of the twentieth century, mentoring took on a very different look and purpose. Most important, research pointed to the worth of mentoring relationships in leadership development. This is a major reason for the many formal programs today, but it is only one.

NEW MENTORING MODELS

Companies are using mentoring programs for a variety of ends, including to:

- *Advance the interests of special groups and populations.* Whereas in the past, members selected protégés who looked, thought, and acted as they did, many of the new organizational mentoring initiatives are designed to help members of select groups rise in the organization. The mentors' purpose is to help women or members of racial, ethnic, and other definable groups upgrade their leadership skills and political savvy and move into managerial positions. A case in point is World Bank, which began a program to help women eager for advancement in Asia in 1997. Now it has several such initiatives. Some programs are region-specific, others are discipline-specific.

- *Support knowledge management.* Mentoring has been found to be an effective way to bring staff together to share knowledge about their jobs. Previous desires to hoard knowledge, skills, and know-how disappears as helping another via mentoring builds goodwill and friendship. Indeed, for this very reason, companies are encouraging a manager to take on more than one mentee and mentees to have more than one advisor—to create not just multiple mentor relationships but a personal board of advisors. Companies believe that, over time, mentoring can create many helping relationships and consequently improve the quality of work life in general and the sharing of best practices in particular.
- *Teach technical skills to the boomers.* While some companies have designed programs that offer an opportunity for techies, number-crunchers, and other IT professionals to develop people and leadership skills under the mentorship of skilled supervisors, others have found that their managers can benefit from learning more about the new office technology and have encouraged partnerships between senior executives and IT professionals. This kind of program has come to be known as *reverse mentoring.* Everyone knows about GE's reverse mentoring program, primarily because Jack Welch, when chairman and CEO, was a key player—as a mentee of a techie. But other companies have taken the idea and found other learning experiences for their senior executives. Procter & Gamble, for instance, has managers in lower-levels of business units act as mentors for those higher up in the business. The mentors are one to two levels below those whom they coach, and the coaching is designed to help these senior executives develop greater self-awareness of their behavior.
- *Prepare expatriates for overseas assignments.* Global firms have experienced managers abroad mentor new recruits with overseas assignments, preparing them for cultural adjustments via e-mail and telephone communications. This is sometimes called distance mentoring or virtual mentoring. The new technology has also facilitated mentoring efforts between employees at different corporate sites or those with busy travel schedules who have more time to carry on private conversations on a plane or in a hotel in a city in which they have a business meeting than meeting at a coffee shop near their office for a quick breakfast or lunch or staying late at the office to catch up on developments in both managers' busy lives.

Of the corporate programs, some do no more than encourage mentor-mentee partnerships while others are much more structured. Let me share some brief descriptions of mentoring programs out there. For instance,

Southwest Airlines involves prospective pilots, as mentees, in its program. Would-be pilots are paired with Southwest pilots. "We want these recruits to hear stories from pilots who have been in their shoes," said Lilah Steen who, with Amy Webb, manages the company's "Take Off" mentoring program for the flight operations recruiting team in Southwest's people (Human Resources) department. "We felt it would help to establish relationships with people while they were in school or gaining the flight time needed to apply here," said Steen. Almost 60 pilots act as mentors. The pilots involved in the program love to talk up the program, according to Webb. If they meet someone who's interested in working for Southwest, they send them to the two coordinators of the firm's "Take Off" program. They may also learn about the "Take Off" program at job fairs. Mentees who already know a Southwest pilot are matched with that pilot if possible. Otherwise, Steen matches the mentee with a pilot who lives in the same area.

United Defense's mentoring effort is designed to help minority and female employees prepare and advance to leadership positions. The organization uses the term *associate* for mentees and its initial program began in 2003 with 20 mentor-associate pairs. The program is developed and run by an implementation team of HR staff and assigned coordinators from each major business group within the organization's armament systems division. Information about the program is communicated via the ASD intranet site, as well as in posters, brochures, and corporate newsletter articles. Like many companies with mentoring programs, United Defense included a one-day seminar on the mentor-associate relationship for the 20 pilot program pairs and a 90-minute orientation for the associates' first-line managers. While it may still be too soon for the firm to crow about the program's success, Ted Kuriata, director-level manager for the program, has expressed optimism. He expects to see the program expand to include satellite manufacturing companies.

Training is an integral element of many of the programs being implemented, thereby demonstrating awareness that there are skills both mentors and mentees need to have for the relationship to work well (see Chapter 1). For instance, Hewlett-Packard's Roseville, California facility has a sitewide program that has mentors and mentees each attend separate half-day training workshops that use written guides, videotapes, and skill practice. American Family Insurance's mentoring program uses a video as part of its training. Facilitators use segments of the video to illustrate points and demonstrate effective mentoring in action. During program evaluations, supervisors of mentees and supervisors of mentors are asked for their impressions of the program and developments on the part of their employees after training.

Why such corporate interest in mentoring? It's all about the return on invested time. At DuPont, the number of minority persons in top management positions rose from 10 percent to 35 percent three years after mentoring was implemented. A Ford plant was able to reduce by 87 percent the time in orientation training for novice engineers due to mentoring. Varian Associates' Radiation Division cut staff turnover in half and also increased productivity through mentoring. Prior to development of its mentoring program, the division had been losing money. It was even being considered for the chopping block. But by the program's fifth year, the division had become a major profit center. GE's Power Generation Division found mentoring to be a good recruitment tool during the past economic boom when it was tough to recruit techies. A Texas Instruments plant found mentoring increased productivity. "The big advantage is mentoring helps employees contribute faster," said one of the program's mentors.

MENTORING IN THE PUBLIC INTEREST

Mentoring programs don't just take place within companies. Increasingly, corporations are encouraging staff to participate in community programs, acting as mentors to college undergraduates, high-potential youngsters in grades 10 through 12, and dropouts from high school, among others. For instance, Eaton Corporation pairs undergrads pursuing BS degrees in electrical, mechanical, industrial, or environmental engineering, or computer science with senior technical people who guide them through the summer season and keep in touch during the school year as well. Hewlett-Packard offers its e-mail mentor to students and teachers in grades 5 through 12 with a focus on helping the students to excel in math and science. Pratt & Whitney Canada, Ltd., offers three mentoring programs for young adults, including one for dropouts and youngsters in trouble who can benefit from extra time with an adult.

As a goal, the Governor's Mentoring Initiative in Florida hopes to recruit over 200,000 Floridians as mentors to help youngsters in school excel. To date, the program has at least 190,000 mentors and over 125,000 young people in the programs. There are 215 companies throughout Florida participating in the program, some extending on-site programs to support the youngsters in their community. Some mentors work face to face with the young adults while others rely on e-mail to provide advice and counsel to the youngsters.

While these programs are growing daily, this book will focus on corporate programs with strategic goals. But the book isn't only about facilitated or structured programs. It is also for those executives and managers who are in or are considering informal mentoring relationships.

BOOK STRUCTURE AND OVERVIEW

The book itself is divided into four parts. In Part One, we look at the mentoring relationship as a process. In the first chapter, you will learn not only how to select a protégé or mentee but also how qualified you are to mentor a protégé. Unfortunately, there are executives and managers who would be toxic to a productive mentoring relationship. We describe those mentor traits dangerous to a successful partnership, as well as describe toxic protégés, rather than have you waste time in mentoring someone who should be left alone.

Chapter 2, "The Three Stages of Mentoring," focuses on the phases that a relationship goes through, and how you can use each stage to build stronger ties with your protégé. This chapter pays particular attention to that first meeting with the mentee, and how to dissolve the relationship when it offers no more worth to either party.

Part Two of the book outlines your responsibilities as a mentor. You already know that as a mentor, you will be a role model, broker, cheerleader, and coach. Chapter 3 explains the first three of these responsibilities and what they entail. Chapter 4 expands on your role as cheerleader and broker with specific skills you need to help your mentee advance in her career. You'll discover career development tricks that you can share with your mentee as well as use yourself to advance in your own career.

Chapter 5, "Straight Talk," focuses on your coaching responsibilities, especially how to give effective constructive feedback. "I don't need help with that," you may want to say. "I've been a supervisor and manager for some time." Maybe, but coaching a mentee is very different from coaching a staff member because positional power plays no part in your role as mentor. Keep in mind that managing someone is very different from mentoring someone, and you'll see how that difference plays out as you coach your mentee.

Chapter 6, "The E-Dimension," introduces you to the impact that the new technology has had on the role of mentor. Increasingly, mentors are communicating via phone and e-mail with mentees. Sometimes, they work at different sites, sometimes in different countries. You'll see how, as a mentor, you can use the new technology effectively to advise and counsel a protégé even when you can't see the impact you are having—there are no visual clues as to how your input is being received because you aren't face to face. This chapter also explores the global dimension of mentorship.

Why do mentors say that the experience makes them better at coaching and counseling? As Chapter 7, "Mentoring through Difficult Situations," demonstrates, mentors may be called upon to give criticism without demoraliz-

ing protégés. This chapter looks at troubles that arise due to a mentee's behavioral problems, which can be tough if the protégé is resistant. It also looks
at problems the team may experience from external influences, like survival
of the partnership during a period of downsizing or coping with the jealousy
of one of the protégé's coworkers. This is a chapter that should be in any
book about counseling troubled workers, although in this instance the troubled workers are both mentors and mentees.

Chapter 8 looks at the pros and cons of a supervisor as a mentor. Assuming that a manager chooses to mentor a staff member, it describes how
to do so as part of a total performance management program.

Chapter 9, the final chapter in Part Two, examines traps to avoid, from
a mentor's perspective. As you'll read, some the problems in the partnership
can be remedied, others may be so problematic that mentor and mentee may
need to find new partners. In formal relationships, it may be time to review
the agreement to see how to end the mentorship.

In Part Three, we look at team mentoring. Chapter 10 shows how managers can mentor a group of employees working as a team, a self-directed
team, or a cross-functional group. In this context, the mentor is more likely
called a "sponsor" than a mentor, although he or she performs all the roles
of a mentor, from role model to advisor, broker, or advocate.

Your firm may be considering a formal program, or it may have one already. In whichever situation you find yourself, you'll find Part Four helpful
because it looks at the how-tos of facilitated or structured programs. Chapter 11 explains what elements your program needs to incorporate to work effectively. It identifies all those elements that are critical to a formal program,
including the importance of a corporate culture that is supportive of mentoring. You'll also discover the pros and cons of participation in such formal
programs versus building your own informal relationships.

Human resources managers and others within an organization who are
considering undertaking a formal program will also find this chapter and
the subsequent chapters worth reading as they develop a corporate program.

Chapter 12, "Selection of a Program Coordinator or Coordinating Committee," shows why a dedicated individual or group is necessary to chivvy participants to persevere in their mentor/mentee relationship. Part of their role
may be to match mentors and mentees and this chapter will offer insights
into how to best do this. A coordinator or coordinating team may want to include the equivalent of an appraisal process that allows mentor and mentee
to assess one another and bring to the surface any problems in the relationship. This chapter explains how such an evaluative program can work.

Chapter 13 looks at negotiating sound mentoring agreements; that is,
how formal programs use agreements between mentors and protégés to set

the stage for a positive mentoring relationship. This agreement can be used in informal relationships as well with a little tweaking by mentor or mentee. Not only does this agreement clarify expectations of both mentor and mentee but it also includes a provision to end relationships without hurting anyone's feelings.

As I mentioned earlier, mentoring today includes cross-gender and cross-cultural structured programs. Chapter 14, "Special Situations," looks at these, as well as peer mentoring, reverse mentoring, and mentoring via a personal advisory board (think three or more mentors at once).

Throughout the book you'll read about structured programs that have begun to grow the next generation of leaders. Some of these programs have other purposes as well, as you will see. From your examination of these programs, you should have some insight into how you might spearhead a formal program within your organization. If you don't believe that the time is right within your company for such a program, then you will welcome the advice in Part Two to make you a more valuable mentor.

1

WHO IS TO BE A MENTOR, WHOM IS TO BE MENTORED?

Before you agree to mentor someone, you should have some insight into what the role demands—both in abilities and responsibilities. Further, unless you will be part of a structured program in which you will be paired by your organization, you should have some insights into what to look for in a mentee or protégé.

M-E-N-T-O-R

Author Beverly Kaye, cofounder and CEO of Career Systems International, has literally defined the role of mentor. She spells it out in the following way, thereby defining the role as well as the word:

- **M** is for model, which reflects a mentor's responsibility to serve as role model as well as point out others who are good role models for her protégé.
- **E** is for encouragement, which is a part of the mentor's role as cheerleader or advocate. As Kaye observes, mentors support their mentees in the risk taking that is essential to their growth.
- **N** is for nurture. A mentor needs to identify his or her mentee's unique skills and capabilities and work with him or her to make the most of these talents.

- **T** is for teacher. Another term might be *coach*. The mentor is responsible for providing constructive feedback.
- **O** is for organization. A mentor is there to lead his or her protégé through the organization, avoiding political minefields.
- **R** is for reality. This may be one of the most important responsibilities of a mentor, for he or she helps a mentee better understand how the organization works—those aspects of the organization that aren't written about in any policy manual. I would add that the mentor also helps to bring reality to a mentor's dreams for the future, creating an action plan that makes them within reach and, sometimes, helping a protégé accept that some goals are only dreams, beyond their reach.

UNDERSTANDING THE MENTOR'S ROLE

Given the increasing number of individuals willing to mentor others, some people would say that it is a relatively easy undertaking. Not so. People have different goals and come from different life experiences. If someone is to mentor another person, that individual must not only be able to offer advice but determine the best help to offer. A protégé doesn't necessarily know the nature of help needed, let alone know the answers to the questions that should be asked.

So, as you can see, being someone's mentor can be challenging. Sometimes, you must be a storyteller, sharing your experience or another's to make a point; at other times, you may have to be an empathetic listener. Occasionally, it's a coach's pep talk that your protégé needs. Further, not only must you know what to say but how to say it and when.

As a mentor, there will also be times when the information you share is sensitive. One mentor I know found himself in the awkward position of having to recommend to an administrative assistant the need both to speak up at meetings and, much more sensitive, undertake an image makeover. The executive appreciated her ability to move ahead, but he knew she wasn't perceived as a manager, despite the fact that she already was doing many managerial tasks. The reason was twofold. First, while she attended managerial meetings as an assistant, she had never taken it upon herself to share her ideas. Rather, she would send e-mail notes to her boss outlining her ideas or prattle off her ideas to him and his peers. These ideas often became the basis of management decisions but the young assistant never received credit.

Addressing this problem entailed coaching the young woman to think through her ideas to conclusion and then prepare her conclusions for presentation to the group. Depending on the nature of the idea, her mentor suggested that she put her proposal in written form. But proposing that she needed not only to act more managerial but also look more managerial was a much more delicate issue to address.

Should such an issue matter? Probably not, but in the real world it does. So the mentor had to raise the issue with his protégé and frame his suggestion in such a manner that she understood the good intentions behind it. As he told her, "You have to dress for the part you want."

Everyone can recall at least one colleague who was technically brilliant and had everything to offer his organization but was derailed because of political blunders, lack of interpersonal skills, ignorance of the unwritten rules, failure to think as a team member, arrogance or insensitivity to others, managing upward instead of down, or some other shortcoming. A mentor's willingness to coach the talented worker or manager—to tell it like it is—could have saved the individual to his benefit and that of the organization.

Coaching a protégé in this manner is one of four key roles that a mentor plays. The other three are role model, cheerleader, and broker. Most attention focuses on the coaching aspects of mentoring but the other three are equally important. All four will be discussed in this book to prepare you as a mentor.

In your role as mentor, you will often lead and sometimes literally follow to observe your protégé, or set up circumstances to have your protégé follow you, situations called "shadowing." Finally, there will be times when you will withdraw, giving your protégé the opportunity to prove himself. This doesn't mean that you leave your protégé to sink or swim. Rather, you give the person the chance to succeed while remaining in the background, ready to offer support if the need arises.

THE COMPLEX SIDE OF MENTORING

So far, it may all sound simple, right? Now let's look at the added complexity. First of all, your role will change depending on the person you mentor. It will be very different if the person is a young adult or an ambitious up-and-comer, a 30-plus workaholic, a cynical baby boomer, or a 58-year-old executive contemplating career options after retirement.

To add further to the complexity, mentoring isn't necessarily linear. All may seem to be going smoothly when your protégés trips over their feet and need further coaching and support. Yes, you'll need to give your protégés space to experiment but you also have to be prepared for them to make mistakes. Sometimes, a protégé will lean too much on you as a mentor and you'll want out of the relationship and it won't be easy. There are also some mentors who don't want to let go. It's not a lot of fun to hear others' problems, but we all love to give advice, and one of the pitfalls of helping another is becoming so involved in their life that we don't want to step away—rather, we want to control the decisions made.

What if the individual is located at another office site and your face-to-face mentoring efforts are few and far between. Much of your communications are electronic, and you won't be able to watch body language or other visible cues to determine how your sage advice is being received, even if it is being considered "sage."

Cultural differences can add further to the communication problems. Multinational organizations have facilitated mentoring programs to enable executives from different operations around the world to be prepared for new foreign assignments via mentoring, which entails skill in intercultural communication—via e-mail most of the time. Given cultural differences, we can be ineffective or, worse, we can inadvertently offend another.

Given the litany of problems you may encounter, then, why should you be a mentor? Despite all of this, mentoring can be rewarding.

WHAT YOU GAIN FROM MENTORING

First and foremost, you'll learn. By serving as a mentor, you'll learn from your mentees. They have knowledge you don't have. They may be able to teach you a new job-specific skill or help you enhance your people-development skills, which you can use with your own staff members.

Mentors tell me that mentoring someone facilitates their own professional growth, making them more of an asset to their organization. "Mentoring helped me strengthen my coaching and leadership skills by working with individuals from different backgrounds and with different personality types," one mentor told me. In this instance, the executive mentored not only a baby boomer but a Gen-Xer. "The experience gave me the ability to supervise people different from me." The mentor is a baby boomer himself. As more Gen-Xers move up, he said, "I will have to work with them. My mentoring experience has better equipped me for this."

Mentoring will also give you a fresh perspective on your own performance. A mentor from a pharmaceutical firm found that her mentee always asked "why"—"Why do this rather than that?" "Why think this way?" "Why take this approach?" The questions, she told me, "helped me to take a critical look at my own performance and what areas I needed to adjust for improvement."

You also will receive recognition from peers and superiors. Being effective at developing another won't go unrecognized by senior management.

Actually, if you are already a member of management, your ability to groom talent may be recognized if you are considered for more authority. If you're a participant in a facilitated program, it's likely that you'll be recognized for your contribution.

You'll get extra work done. Mentees also will want to pay you back for your counsel and support and will willingly assist you with a project if the need arises. Some of this help can even become learning experiences for your mentee—so you both benefit. Isn't there a project group that needs help but you just don't have enough time? This may be a perfect opportunity for your mentee.

You can shorten learning curves for new employees. This is a real benefit if you are the individual's supervisor. A new recruit with high-potential is the perfect person to get a little extra coaching and nurturing (think "mentoring") so the recruit pulls his or her weight and more, maybe some of your own. A talented staff member may be mentored by you as part of a performance management approach, and the added time should allow you to assign your new recruit tasks you might otherwise have to do and thereby free you to take on other critical tasks. There are pros and cons about mentoring your own staff mentors, so you'll want to read Chapter 8, "Supervisor as Mentor."

As a mentor, not only will you be able to communicate the company's values—values having to do with quality of customer service, the kinds of relationships expected among coworkers, the sense of teamwork expected of everyone, and shared responsibility for corporate profitability—but you will be able to share your values. Imagine how excited you will be when you see what impact your beliefs have had on some up-and-coming person.

Let me share with you a story to illustrate the excitement that may be yours from creating an exceptional learning experience for your protégé. This is a true story. The founder of the successful newspaper *USA TODAY* wrote about it in his autobiography *Confessions of an S.O.B.* (Doubleday, 1989).

Allen Neuharth had been taken under the wing of Lee Hill, executive editor of the *Detroit Free Press*. He was Hill's assistant, and one day, Hill invited Neuharth to join him for lunch with Jack Knight, owner of the Knight-Ridder newspaper chain. Expecting that he would be eating at some posh restaurant, he found himself in the basement lunch counter of an old Woolworth's. Knight ordered a hot dog and then asked Neuharth what he wanted. Neuharth had the same.

Yes, it was exciting to meet a man like Knight, wherever they ended up lunching, but the advice that came from Knight and what he subsequently learned from Hill was felt to be even more helpful in his career. Knight told Neuharth that working with Lee Hill—and, as assistant, being privy to his thinking (think mentee)—would give him access to Detroit's mayor and a lot of other civic leaders, and entrance into the Detroit Club and other select eateries. But Knight warned Neuharth that there would be a danger of making the wrong assumption that he was writing for the people he met at these locales. Knight reminded the young man that many more of his readers ate at coffee shops and counters like they were then at. "Keep your feet on the street. Don't eat at the Detroit Club every day."

Neuharth attributed that experience into his thinking years later about the creation of a popular national tabloid that was *USA TODAY.*

Finally, you can learn from your own protégé. Just as you can help your protégé see himself or herself as others do, in time trust will develop between you and your protégé so he or she will feel confident in offering insights about which of your management and leadership skills could benefit from mentoring by another.

Note that I focused on those benefits to you—not to the protégé or your organization. Mentoring is a win-win-win relationship, but if you are to make the commitment to help by being a mentor to someone, and mentoring does take time, you should be clear about the benefits to you personally.

Mentees will benefit from your job and career advice, from insights into how the organization *really* operates, access to valuable contacts, and constructive feedback. Your organization will benefit from better performance from you and your mentee, from lower turnover and easier recruitment, and the next generation of leaders that you contribute to creating as a mentor. But before you commit to an informal relationship or participate in a formal program, identify the benefits for yourself. Indeed, you might even want to make a list of how the experience as guide, listener, coach, and even friend can open the door for you. One mentor told me, "When I help my mentee achieve something special and important to them. I feel I've made a powerful investment in our organization's most valuable asset—its people." Another told me, "I never dreamed how much I knew that was special to me until I began to mentor a technician in the organization. Things I had observed or reasoned out, but never wrote down, kept coming back to me as his needs kept popping up." Better yet, let me share some mentee feedback about their experience. It says much about what's in it for you as a mentor: "When I came to really know my mentor, I knew I'd not feel alone again as long as there were people like her in the organization. I've learned to trust more and to take charge of my future through her help." And, "I never dreamed that I could learn so much in so little time. His insights into the nature of the organization, how it works, and what it rewards, will, I'm sure, make an enormous difference in my career."

HOW A MENTORING RELATIONSHIP SUCCEEDS

There are elements that are important to an informal and structured program, but most important may be the traits and characteristics, as well as knowledge and understanding, of the mentors and protégés who will be paired.

A mentor must be more than someone who is good at his or her job and well connected. A good corporate track record with the firm won't hurt but it, too, isn't enough. Nor is an understanding of the politics of the organization. It is someone willing to make a commitment of time and attention to help others' develop. You might say that those who make good mentors, like the early astronauts, have the "right stuff." This isn't to say that they are motivated solely by the altruistic experience. Many mentors have told me that being a mentor gives them deeper insights into the people with which they are paired.

In many ways, protégés or mentees, too, need the right stuff. When choosing someone to be mentored, you need to look for several traits, including a willingness to learn, openness to input, ambition, and promise within the organization. They may be taken under the wing of one of the company's executives but, at the same time, they have to accept responsibility for their own career development.

To understand what makes a mentoring relationship work, it is worthwhile to look at a successful one. In this instance, Bob, office manager, had chosen to take Faith, buyer for the firm, under his wing. He had reason to do so.

Faith had a track record that showed that she was willing to assume responsibility for her own growth and development. Right out of high school, she had started with the organization as a receptionist. She had also enrolled in a community college program, during which she demonstrated strong skills in business finance. While Faith was good with other people, she also enjoyed the excitement that came with bargaining with others and winning. So, Faith's advisor recommended she work toward a bachelor of science degree in business. As she did this, an opening for an assistant occurred in the purchasing department. Faith applied and got the job. As such, she demonstrated her willingness to work hard and late into the night, her understanding of people, and her initiative in investigating costs for her boss. Consequently, when one of the firm's buyers moved on, Faith was given the job.

The head of purchasing did not see development of staff as a critical role for him, so he welcomed Bob's interest in her work. When Faith saved Bob's department several thousand dollars by careful study of several suppliers of office furnishings, Bob had taken interest in Faith's future. He spent time talking to her about her career, and he learned that she wanted to be more than the firm's purchasing manager—she wanted a position in finance. This meant a major career shift.

Bob knew that Faith needed more than training in financial management—a ghetto kid, she lacked the social skills that would get her the attention of senior management. Helping Faith get approval from senior management to work toward a master's degree in finance was simpler than helping Faith understand how her manner would also influence her career. He pointed to one or two women in the organization as role models, and he had her participate in a task project with him where she could learn not to be as tough on her coworkers as she was on vendors who came to sell the company something.

As Faith completed her financial management training, Bob sought one experience after another from which Faith could learn and also gain the attention of others in the organization. When she received her master's degree, she also was transferred into accounting where she shined among the number-crunchers. Inevitably, she moved swiftly up the career ladder to chief financial officer and ultimately to vice president of finance.

By then, Bob had retired. But he kept in close touch with friends from the company and was proud of the legacy he had left the company.

What made Faith such a good mentee? The answer is multifaceted but clear.

- She had a track record of success.
- She had demonstrated her intelligence and initiative in her jobs.
- She was loyal to the organization and committed to its values.
- She shared with Bob a desire to achieve results.
- She enjoyed challenges and willingly accepted greater responsibility.
- She took responsibility for her own career advancement and growth. Yes, Bob advised, but she planned the action steps that would lead to her ultimate goal.
- She valued feedback even on those occasions when it wasn't positive. She realized that she could make mistakes, but rarely did she repeat them because she listened to and followed the advice more experienced individuals gave her.
- She welcomed Bob's help in smoothing out her rough edges, as much as she did his help in better understanding the political side of the organization.

AN EXCELLENT MENTOR

What made Bob such a good mentor?

He had strong interpersonal skills. Bob liked to work with people. He also had good communication skills, which meant he was not only articulate but an active listener. A practitioner of the 80/20 rule, he listened 80 percent of the time and only talked about 20 percent in most communications with his staff members. He knew how to ask open-ended questions—that is, questions that require more than yes or no answers—and he listened to the responses, nodding and moving toward the speaker in a manner that demonstrated he wanted to hear more. He then paraphrased what he had been told to ensure that he understood what the other party said.

Rather than answer all Faith's questions, Bob also found it worthwhile to ask her more questions to force her to think through situations and come up with the right answers herself.

Bob had contacts both within and outside the organization. Although he was only office manager, he had tremendous influence within the company—based on the loyalty he had gained by helping others once or twice when they needed his help. He knew the organization well and was able to share with Faith insights about the company's long-range goals and strategic intent he had gained from the movers and shakers within the organization. This knowledge allowed her to identify those who might be obstacles to completing the projects assigned her and to develop plans to gain the support of these individuals. Consequently, she was able to develop an impressive track record once she got to the finance department, thereby attracting the attention of senior management.

Bob recognized others' accomplishments. He had learned how motivating this could be. So he went out of his way to acknowledge the accomplishments of those with whom he worked. He never took credit for the work of his employees. But neither did he praise them unless it was deserved—because he understood that praise that is not legitimately earned has little or no value—it even undermines the value of the giver.

His credibility meant that comments he made about the quality of Faith's work were taken seriously.

He was good at supervising people. Faith wasn't one of his staff members, but the same skill that he used in delegating tasks to his employees was used in defining the work he expected her to assume that would position her for advancement. A good mentor is someone who manages people successfully.

He accepted the risk that came with mentoring. There is no guarantee that each time a mentee steps outside her box she will be successful. A mentor has to have the courage to know that the person he is sponsoring may sometimes fail and to be willing to be there to support that person should she be beyond her depths. A mentor is someone who says enthusiastically to the mentee, "Go to it!" but who also is prudent about the risks he lets the employee take on. After all, the mentor wants the mentee not only to build new skills but also to increase her self-confidence from a stream of wins.

Bob is willing to be available to help another advance in the organization. He was willing to commit both his time and emotional energy to Faith because he felt she was worth the effort. He wasn't threatened by the thought that one day Faith might even surpass him professionally. He realized he could move her career forward by sharing with her the "unwritten rules" about the organization, wisdom he had gained the hard way from breaking the rules himself. But if he hadn't, Faith could easily have been a bull in a china shop in trying to complete the projects Bob arranged for her to assume.

During his meetings, Bob also had to listen to her insecurities and help her answer "What if . . ." questions. He had to let her test ideas, listen to them objectively, advise on the wisdom of pursuing them, help her adapt them as appropriate and then help her to present the idea to others in the best light.

In short, he had to be willing to devote time to Faith's career—two hours every two weeks or four hours a month. More than this would have been too much, making Faith overdependent on Bob. On the other hand, even four hours, given the time pressures on most managers, represent a major commitment. After all, four hours are the equivalent of one team meeting, two vendor interviews, two lunches with his own boss, or a review of a stack of demands from corporate managers for approval. Regardless, it was a commitment Bob had to keep.

Consider what might have happened if Bob had not kept his promise to meet with Faith regularly over lunch to discuss her progress, even if he had had legitimate reasons for not being available. It's likely it would have done just the opposite of what he intended: His superstar's performance would have faded.

Put yourself in Bob's shoes. Think about those within your organization. Identify someone with equivalent qualifications to those of Faith, someone who can benefit from the following:

- *Knowledge and skills.* Under the tutelage of a sound mentor, a mentee can avoid trial-and-error mistakes.
- *Coaching, advice, guidance, and support.* In other words, you would be a mentee's personal coach. You would be that person to whom your mentee could go to for information, idea testing, and advice.

- *Understanding of organizational culture and politics.* You could teach your mentee appropriate behavior and protocol—how to get things done within the organizational framework.
- *New opportunities and contacts.* You would open doors for your mentee, providing new opportunities (for instance, to attend an important meeting, give a presentation, or take on a new and challenging assignment). You could also introduce your mentee to new contacts—people who could advance a career.
- *Greater career success.* Ultimately, the previously mentioned benefits result in greater career success. That's what happened to Faith.

You do this by the following:

- Setting high expectations
- Teaching by example
- Offering wise counsel
- Showing a genuine interest in your protégé
- Demonstrating a sense of humor
- Inspiring and encouraging the protégé
- Having a willingness to accept another's viewpoint
- Exhibiting patience and kindness
- Offering secrets into how the company really works
- Providing learning experiences
- Taking time to hear your mentee out
- Challenging behavior and rerouting thinking in more productive directions

You may be a cool guy or gal within the organization, but your responsibility as a mentor is to coach, listen, and guide your mentee. You promise to keep confidential your conversations and you keep your promise. You are honest and truthful in your communication. You promise to make yourself available X times per month and you are there for the mentee X times a month. You don't enter into a mentoring relationship with any of the following attitudes:

- *I will always be there for the protégé.* Too much help can make your mentee overdependent on you.
- *I know best.* Some executives enter into mentoring relationships because they enjoy being recognized as someone in the know. They like the compliments their contributions get. They are less concerned about their protégé's needs, and consequently won't offer other opportuni-

ties for their mentee to learn from others knowledgeable in areas they aren't.

- *I'm there to help my mentee get ahead.* That's great, but it's important to clarify for the mentee what that really means. No one—even a dedicated mentor—can guarantee advancement in today's fast-changing business world. All you can do is be your protégé's cheering squad, using your credibility within the organization to give your mentee the visibility necessary for his or her capabilities to get noticed by those who make decisions about promotions.

Think about those you have met during your career who have invested a little extra time in you. Use these individuals as models for your own mentoring role. Indeed, list those who served as mentors, maybe unaware to both of you. Even as I write this list, I can't help but think of an associate who always found time to hear my concerns, my ideas, and my desires, who brought my thinking to the attention of others in his organization, and who gave me sound advice. Until this moment, I hadn't realized that he was one of the helpers in my life—a mentor.

SHOULD YOU BE A MENTOR?

Ask yourself these 15 questions. While there is no "ideal profile" of a mentor, needless to say, the more questions to which you can answer yes, the more likely it is that you will make an outstanding mentor.

1. Do I enjoy working with other people?
2. Am I a good listener who demonstrates respect for my colleagues?
3. Am I sensitive to the needs and feelings of others?
4. Do I recognize when others need support? What about being given free reign?
5. Is it enough to find reward in service to someone who can benefit from my experience and knowledge?
6. Am I flexible and willing to adjust my business schedule to meet the needs of someone else?
7. Am I able to help another person without smothering him or her?
8. Am I patient and tolerant when teaching someone?
9. Am I confident and secure in my know-how and do I make an effort to remain up to date?
10. Do I set high standards for myself and my staff? Would I do the same for a mentee?

11. Do others look to me for information about my area of expertise?
12. Do I enjoy my work and want to share that excitement and challenge with others?
13. Am I able to explain things to others regardless of complexity?
14. Do I have the self-confidence sufficient to help someone move ahead without feeling threatened?
15. Are others interested in my ideas and opinions?

WHAT TO MENTOR

We have discussed who should serve as mentor, and what qualities to look for in a mentee. But as a prospective mentor, what subjects should be the focus of your efforts? I suggest you begin with the following three:

1. *Job fundamentals.* While you want to help your mentee acquire knowledge in general, you should also identify those competencies or skills, abilities, and knowledge that the mentee lacks that could help with the current job or the job he or she wants to have next.

W h a t   M a k e s   B a d   M e n t o r s

Before you decide to take on the responsibility of a mentor, assess not only your best qualities but your poor ones. The following are traits that disqualify you as a mentor:

- Too dictatorial—intolerant of others' mistakes
- Like to be in control, in the limelight
- Very poor at keeping in touch
- Take no interest in others' aspirations
- Judgmental
- Disloyal, unlikely to keep confidences
- Unapproachable, hard to approach
- Very poor communicator
- Poor in keeping commitments; make time for things but then abandon for something else you deem more important
- Very biased viewpoint and not willing to consider others' points of view

2. *Leading.* Your mentee's position on the organizational chart doesn't matter. As decision making is lowered and organizations experience accelerating change, it is critical that all staff members possess leadership ability. The more leadership knack a mentee has, the more responsibility he can take in achieving your organization's mission and undertaking strategic plans. Keep that in mind. An administrative assistant may have fewer leadership tasks than your CEO, but both have leadership responsibilities.

3. *Relationship building.* Interpersonal skills are only the beginning. Mentees must be able to relate to all within the organization and outside of it—to overcome conflicts and build collaborative relationships.

What Makes You Want to Be a Mentor?

For each of the statements below, put a check under Yes if the reason reflects why mentoring appeals to you. If it does not, put a check in the No column. The list reflects many of the reasons executives and managers choose to mentor others, either informally or formally. Too many checks in the No column may suggest that you should rethink your interest in mentoring someone.

Reasons That Mentoring Appeals to You   Yes   No

I like to give others advice or guidance.

I find that helping others is personally rewarding.

I have knowledge that I want to share with others.

I find working with others who are younger or from another discipline energizing.

I see mentoring furthering my own growth as well as that of the mentee.

C a s e S t u d y

PUTTING MENTORING INTO THE HANDS OF MENTEES

In the past, Agilent Technologies assigned mentors to mentees (think "forced matching"). But that didn't work for the company. As Patricia Chapman, of the firm's New Generation Leadership program, explained, "If you assume that a young working mother would want a woman mentor who's been successful in that aspect of her working life, you might be totally wrong. The young woman may have different goals for her mentoring, and she should make the choice for herself."

With the assistance of The Mentoring Group, the company decided to provide participants with a list of qualified mentors and the ability to choose from the list. The database lists people identified as ideal mentors against set criteria. The mentors register themselves into the database, indicating their background and areas of expertise. Mentees can enter information to describe what they're looking for in a mentor and then search for matches.

Chapman explained that the mentees "own" the search and selection process. They actually call the mentors themselves. "These high-potential mentees have a lot of initiative, and they're assertive. It may seem a little intimidating to drive a relationship with a top-level mentor, but it helps the mentee improve his or her negotiating skills."

The company gives the mentees guidelines on how to contract with their new mentor. Consequently they go to a mentor knowing exactly what they want to work on and how much time they want. "It's a springboard for conversation." The organization uses quantitative and qualitative data gathered from pre-surveys and post-surveys, as well as 360-degree surveys, to evaluate how well people have improved their leadership skills in the Next Generation Leadership program.

According to Chapman, the program has been effective. Ninety percent of participants say so. This high level of success is attributed to a decision by the firm to reduce the cycle from one year to six months. Mentoring partners are less likely to stop working together if you give them six months, according to Chapman. They don't put things off on the belief that they have plenty of time. Further, to keep the momentum going, participants are encouraged to meet at least two hours per month. It can be four half-hour meetings or one two-hour meeting, but they should spend at least 120 minutes together.

(continued)

The firm believes that face-to-face contact is ideal for mentoring relation-ships, but they do have some long-distance mentoring. "We encourage people to select a mentor they can meet sometime in person. If they have a business reason to travel, perhaps they can arrange to meet their mentor."

Another recent development by the program is a decision to try group mentoring where some mentors have three or four mentees each. Because staff members prefer one-on-one mentoring, these mentors often meet with their mentees one at a time.

2

THE THREE STAGES OF MENTORING

The most successful mentorships are those that are built on a shared understanding of both parties' expectations from the relationship, positive feelings about one another, and a lot of optimism about how the relationship will benefit them both. To some people, this first phase in a mentoring relationship is considered the most important. I personally think that the subsequent stages in the relationship may be as important, if not more important. A mentorship evolves over time, and each stage brings its own rewards and places unique demands on the mentor and mentee.

Let's consider the stages that you and your mentee will go through to see why I say this.

STAGE I

The first stage might be termed the startup phase. Initial meetings lay the foundation for the relationship. But creation of a trusting relationship requires time and dedicated effort. We may be tempted to hurry the process but doing so cheats us of valuable mentoring experiences and decreases the likelihood that the relationship will succeed.

Many mentors assume that the first stage ends as soon as you and the mentee have agreed on career and development goals, clarified expectations, and made arrangements to maintain regular contact. Not so. The first stage can last as long as a year.

During this phase, you, as the mentor, might be esteemed or respected, unable to make any mistake, in the opinion of your mentee. Your mentee will believe that he is cared for, supported, and respected by someone who is admired by the rest of the organization, whether it is so or not. It's great for the ego, however.

Likewise, you will think of your mentee as someone who is easily coached, who is a pleasure to work with, and who will be a professional success with your assistance. If the mentee shows a willingness to lend a hand when you need it, your mentee will be someone you can't praise enough—a paragon of virtues.

These positive feelings will coincide with positive expectations on both sides. You will offer the development opportunities your mentee needs, and your mentee will increasingly look to you for guidance and support. Your mentee may begin to think that you are capable of getting him promoted, and you will start to believe that you are infallible, just as your mentee seems to think.

If you are fortunate, circumstances will be such that you both fulfill the expectations of the other. An opportunity to work on a high visibility project will be seen by your mentee as evidence of your advocacy of his ability, and your mentee's assistance on a critical project that saves the day will convince you that you chose well in a mentee.

But the reality may be very different. Your advice may not always be trusted or followed. The mentee's willingness to lend a hand may be more due to what he hopes to gain from you in the way of a key assignment or, better, a promotion than a show of initiative or gratefulness for the feedback offered—which can come as a surprise but is really immaterial as long as the help is forthcoming.

Whatever happens, during this stage you should come away with new insights into how to coach without positional power, stronger communication skills, and a few extra projects done without having to work every weekend to finish them. Your mentee should have the information and valuable feedback to better position himself for advancement.

As long as you both seem to be getting what you expected from the relationship, there should be no reason for either of you to complain. Also, the positive feelings during this early stage of the relationship are likely to push you on to the second stage. It's during this phase that expectations will be tested against reality.

If you are a television fan as I am, you may recall the long-lived TV series, *MacGyver*. Richard Dean Andersen, as MacGyver, was the star of the show, but he also was the mentee. Costar Dana Elcar played the role of Pete, who was MacGyver's boss and also his mentor. As I see reruns of the show, I can see how the writers allowed the seven-year relationship between these two characters to evolve—from their first adventure together, to a point in MacGyver's career when he questioned continuing to work for Pete, to the time he left Pete to ride off into the sunset on a motorcycle.

As you watch the program, you can see the ups and downs of these two characters, very similar to the ups and downs that occur in real life between mentors and mentees.

STAGE 2

The second stage can last a few months or a few years, depending on how the relationship unfolds. It's during this stage that you and your mentee begin to discover the real benefits of your mentorship.

You will be providing challenging work for your mentee, especially projects with high visibility, as well as serving as her cheerleader or advocate. Your network of contacts will be accessible to her as well. You should see a change in your mentee's behavior, brought about in part by her modeling herself after you and those whose style you have pointed out. Friendship between you and your mentee may evolve from your schedule of regular meetings, including an occasional lunch or dinner meeting. The positive results between you and your mentee will be determined both by your ability to influence your mentee's career in the organization—that is, your rank and experience—and the feelings of trust you share.

Admittedly, how successful you and the mentee are during this stage that some call "the cultivation period" will depend on your mentee's potential, the knowledge and experience you can offer, and the mentee's willingness to reciprocate by being of assistance to you. You may feel fulfilled that you are having a positive influence on the mentee's development if there is evidence of improvement. The mentee will see a change in the respect in which she is held due to your support and nurturing.

It would be wonderful if I could say that this phase continues indefinitely, with you and your mentee both gaining from the relationship. Unfortunately, that isn't always so. Problems can arise. Some can be due to external circumstances. Others may be due to your ability as a mentor.

Within your organization, decisions may be made over which you may have no influence. Cutbacks in staff may involve your mentee who mistakenly may have felt she was immune due to her relationship with you. Even a change in duties might be held against you if new responsibilities aren't seen by the mentee as something she wanted or something that might directly or indirectly lead to advancement. If your position is affected negatively, and you lose your positional power and therefore your ability to influence your mentee's career, your mentee may be more upset for herself than for you. If you sense this, it might impact your feelings toward your mentee.

Let's consider a brighter outlook. Let's assume that your mentee is given new, more important responsibilities, or you benefit from reorganization. If the mentee moves up or into a new career path, he may begin to wonder how worthwhile the current relationship with you is. While you may see your mentee's increased power as helpful to you, giving you access to information and resources you previously might have lacked, your mentee may be too focused on his new responsibilities to want to continue the reciprocal relationship.

At the very least, you will expect gratitude from your mentee, and it may not be forthcoming. Like a proud parent, you would want to feel as if you had contributed to your mentee's success and that she acknowledges that, but, instead, she may see her success as due primarily to her own capabilities and hard work, with an occasional hand from you.

In your new position, you may have access to the help that your mentee provided earlier in the relationship, and you may wonder, given your new responsibilities, if you have sufficient time to provide the help your mentee needs. Alternatively, as you and your mentee move up, you may become more critical of your mentee's skills, ability, and knowledge.

You may both find cause not to be available to meet with each other. Or one of you may need more verbal support than the other, and the other may withdraw as it consumes too much time.

Needless to say, I've drawn a pretty negative scenario here. For some partners, the relationship during this phase may be far richer than anticipated, and the interpersonal bond stronger and more meaningful. But it is important as you enter into a mentoring relationship that you realize that over time changes will occur between you and your protégé, and you need to be prepared for what those changes might bring. So be mindful that problems can occur. Indeed, periodically, check out the health of the relationship. Make sure the needs of your mentee are being satisfied. Likewise, ensure your own needs are satisfied.

In her book *The Mentor's Guide,* consultant Lois J. Zachary makes a key comment: "When mentoring partners regularly discuss their mentoring relationship, the conversation helps to maintain the momentum of the relationship and contributes value to the learning of each partner." Although you, as mentor, may be uneasy about raising tough questions during this period, it may be the ideal time to question the mentee about your effort. If there are problems in the relationship, they may still be small enough to solve. All that may be needed are some midcourse corrections to circumvent major mentoring pitfalls. A mentoring relationship that was moving quickly downhill can be revitalized if concerns are raised soon enough.

If nothing is done to monitor the quality of the mentoring interaction, you and your mentee may more quickly enter the third and final stage.

STAGE 3

During this stage, both you and your mentee may find yourselves moving apart. Your mentee may be demonstrating more independence or, worse, may have grown dependent on you. Neither makes for a positive mentoring relationship and, as a mentor, you know that you must do something. You may begin to look around and see others within the organization with high potential who could benefit from your guidance and counsel. Unconsciously, you may find yourself giving up some of your time to these newbies whom you see as needing the same kind of early mentoring that you initially provided to your protégé.

Your mentee may also be networking within the organization, building relationships with others who can help in areas in which you are not strong. You may still have something to offer your mentee but it may be not as significant, so time spent with you will diminish.

Neither one of you may want to admit a lack of need for the other, so you may continue to meet. But, too often, you may find yourselves talking, not about career or office issues, but about family, hobbies, and the like. In informal relationships, mentors tell me that they really don't know how to put an end to the mentorship. One individual told me that, looking at the situation after the fact, he realized that he could have gone on mentoring a junior executive until his own retirement if the mentee hadn't been offered an assignment outside of the country. "It gave us both a way to say goodbye without offending the other," he told me.

This may explain why mentors in structured programs welcome the use of agreements. These documents, as you'll learn later in the book, generally include clauses that allow for separation when the need for support from the mentor either ceases to exist or problems in the relationship make the time spent together unproductive (see Chapter 9, "Traps to Avoid").

This period of separation can be emotionally upsetting for both you and your mentee. This is particularly true when either you or your protégé see the separation as premature. Mentors who have felt stalled in their own careers tell me that they felt resentful of their mentee's continued opportunities for professional growth. Young mentees, on the other hand, felt unprepared to meet their new career challenges.

The good news is that the ill-feelings that sometimes accompany the separation phase usually disappear. As the mentee finds a new mentor and the mentor accepts a new protégé, both begin to look on their relationship with a new perspective. Based on comments from first-time mentors, if this is your first time taking someone under your wing, you should feel a sense of accomplishment and pride. While you may no longer be perceived as infallible—your pedestal will no longer exist in the mind of your former mentee—your protégé will still feel indebted to you.

As I write this, I am a bit worried that taking the sugar coating away from describing your mentorship may drive you away from the idea. I hope not. Mentors tell me that their mentorships were some of the best things they did for their careers and the careers of the mentees—well worth the hardship that usually accompanies the evolution the relationship goes through. As all the fantasies associated with you and your mentee disappear, the experiences that you share should lead to a new relationship—one of friendship.

However, it is important that you recognize that your mentorship will come to an end at some point, no matter how much you may want to avoid it. Mentors and mentees who have difficulty with relationship endings are those most likely to have difficulty coping with the end of their mentorship. For those, their relationship may be hanging on by a thread, but they would rather that thread remain indefinitely. But it is better to be proactive. As you see the relationship eroding, it is better to discuss and plan how you will come to closure. Set ground rules for having this discussion, one of which may be that you both agree to end the relationship on good terms. Many structured programs include agreements with a no-fault clause that means that neither party is allowed to blame the other if the relationship has to end.

Another rule to consider is one that doesn't force either partner to remain in the relationship if the other wants to break it off. Most often, it will be you, as mentor, who will question continuation of the relationship, so it is important that you make this condition clear from the start of your mentorship.

THE REALITIES

Needless to say, it is easier to end mentoring relationships built on a few brief meetings than it is to say *finis* to a long-term relationship with an exceptional staff member with whom you have probably built a good rapport.

In a short relationship, you can continue to show interest but also look for opportunities for the mentee to meet with and seek answers from others in the organization. In time, you will find that the employee comes to you for help less frequently—and, ultimately, sees you occasionally in the hallway or at social affairs but otherwise is preoccupied with the new mentor.

If your relationship has been long, and you believe that it is time to separate, you should explain your decision to end the mentorship with your mentee. The individual needs to know why you feel you can no longer continue to contribute to his career advancement. For instance, you might point to those development gaps that the employee still has and the skills that a new mentor must have to help close them—areas in which you are not expert. Better yet, you can reassure your mentee that your personal help is no longer needed. Together with your mentee, you can develop a list of prospective new mentors that have the strengths he or she now needs. If the mentee has the talents that brought you together in the first place, it should be easy for you to find another mentor or for the mentee to locate one.

If there are real problems in the relationship, like the traps I will be telling you about later in this book, you may want to discuss them, although their mention could create pleas on your mentee's part to be given another chance. If that is a worry, focus on the growth that will come from a new mentorship.

Even when you end the relationship with a mentee, you should make it clear to the employee that your door is always open for those times that the manager or employee needs help. You also should keep that promise.

LIFE AFTER BEING MENTORED

Mentors with whom I spoke told me that the best way to break up with a mentee is over a special meal together or a drink after work. The occasion needs to be marked as important, for it is a rite of passage—a time to celebrate the mentee's next step on the career rung with the help of a new mentor. Closure is needed between you both. Without it, adjustment can be difficult.

Ideally, find a time and place when you can share stories and laughter. Your mentee needs your blessing and your good wishes. This isn't the time to offer further advice—only to share your optimism about future professional success. Later in this book, you will learn how effective statements and questions are to solving problems. The decision that both you and your mentee move on is a problem of sorts, and it is best handled with a statement—"We've had a great time"—followed by some "recall questions" that help bridge the past to the future: "You wrote lots of proposals while we were together. Will you be doing more of that?" "Remember when you had a major supervisory problem. Do you expect to be hiring new people in the future?" And so forth. Listen to your mentee just like you first listened when you began your relationship—indeed, listen as you might listen to your own mentor. If you are separating because your mentee no longer needs your advice and counsel, your former mentee may, indeed, have experience and knowledge he or she can now share with you.

Before you make a final decision, however, you may want to revisit your purpose. What were your goals in working together? Is there another step you can take together? Let's assume that you both agree that there may be life still left in the old relationship. Even then, you may want to establish a process for acknowledging the time for splitting up. Ask yourself, "How will we know when it is the right time to bring the relationship to an end?" Wouldn't it be great if you can part at a time when your protégé can experience a positive career experience?

What if you were right all along—that is, your relationship is over?

THE DAY AFTER

All right, the relationship is over. Does that mean that you avoid your former mentee? Not at all. But it also means that you don't call before the week is out to see how the mentee is doing. Certainly, you don't inquire about your mentee's new mentor. Allow for weaning.

Your protégé needs to be his or her own person. That means that you have to look on from a distance as your protégé basks in the limelight of future successes. A mentor told me once, "I was so proud of my mentee's promotion to senior VP. I didn't realize that I was walking around the office acting like a new father. It took a third party to make me aware that I was making my former protégé feel uncomfortable."

Just as building rapport is an essential ingredient to starting a successful mentorship, a sense of adjournment is important to letting go. It isn't likely to be comfortable for either you or your mentee, but it's a necessary step in the continued growth and development of your mentee.

In the next section of this book, you are going to learn more about being a mentor—your role and responsibilities, the skills and abilities critical to your success, the kinds of situations you may encounter and how to address them, and much more.

Signs That You Should Part

- You are bored, thinking about other things when you meet your mentee.
- Your mentee shows up on the scheduled date, and you meet whether or not there is an agenda.
- You begin to begrudge the time you must spend to maintain your partnership. You have begun to think that you have more important and pressing issues to which you should attend.
- You feel as if your mentee is becoming codependent and you will never get rid of him or her.
- You have run out of things to discuss with your mentee.
- There has been a breach of confidence—either by you or your mentee.
- Your mentee has begun to listen to but not follow your advice.
- Despite regular meetings, the mentee doesn't seem to be making any professional progress—and you think the mentee blames it on you.
- Your meetings with your protégé tire you yet you don't think you are accomplishing anything.
- You are finding meeting with your mentee unpleasant.

The Quality of Your Mentorship

The following questions will enable you to think about the quality of your relationship with your protégé. They prompt you to express feelings that you may not know exist, as well as identify action strategies you can implement to improve the quality of your mentoring relationship.

1. If you had to describe your mentoring relationship, what words or phrases would you use?

2. How would you describe the interaction when you and your mentee get together?

3. If you had to put a number on your relationship, 1 for least productive and 5 for most productive, which number would you choose?   1 2 3 4 5

   Why? _____

   Put yourself in your mentee's shoes, which number do you think he would choose?
   1 2 3 4 5

   Why?_____

(continued)

4. Do you feel you are getting out of the mentoring relationship what you expected? Yes No

   If no, explain why:

   _____

   _____

5. Do you think your mentee is achieving the goals set early in the relationship? Yes No

   If no, explain why:

   _____

   _____

6. What action strategies should you take to improve the quality of your relationship with your protégé?

   1.

   2.

   3.

L *aying* a F *oundation* *of* T *rust*

Mentors can help a protégé grow and become ready to take on a new position, but they aren't there to help the individual get a new job, either within the organization or outside. During your first meeting as mentor to someone, you need to make that clear. You might add that you can't protect your protégé from change within the organization, whether it is reorganization or downsizing.

At that time, you will have to clearly define your role. As a mentor, you are there to help guide the protégé in making decisions, not to make the decisions for him or her. Finally, you aren't available to coddle your protégé—to provide a comfort zone in which the mentee can feel free to criticize peers or cry on your shoulder about self-esteem problems. Your role is to help come up with ways to address these interpersonal issues by asking insightful questions, serving as a sounding board for ideas, and generally encouraging the mentee to stretch goals and fully utilize potential.

A protégé should go away from those first meetings with a mentor with the knowledge that the individual will be there to enhance development but he or she doesn't guarantee the individual's success—that's the protégé's responsibility in the relationship. The protégé can achieve that by being curious and open to learning from the mentor.

You, too, should go away from those first meetings feeling comfortable about the commitment. Be honest with yourself. If you find yourself drawn into an informal relationship with someone who shows great promise as a leader but could use a little guidance, ask yourself if you would prefer mentoring someone who is new to the field. Alternatively, if faced with someone relatively new to the job market, would you prefer to help someone with more experience but who is unaware of his or her full potential?

Understanding what you could offer as a mentor will help you enter this relationship more positively.

Your First Meeting

Some first-time mentors will hurry through the initial meeting as a result of either discomfort or a busy workday, thereby cheating themselves out of truly getting to know their mentee and, worse, endangering the mentoring relationship. You want to leave your first meeting with the individual with some knowledge about his or her life, career, and career aspirations. This is the case whether the relationship is formal or informal. You may also want to learn if you know any people in common. This will give you a resource for additional information about your mentee as well as someone to talk with about your initial impression of the individual. Such impressions aren't always accurate, and you may want to get a second opinion from someone who has known the prospective mentee longer. This can be helpful whether the mentee left you with a positive or a negative impression.

Keep in mind that the more you know your protégé, the stronger the trust will be between you.

People ask me if both mentor and mentee should experience a kind of chemistry that suggests that the relationship will be successful after their first meeting. The truth is that such positive feelings aren't necessary. Actually, a mentor and a mentee don't even have to like one another. However, they should both be respectful of the other. Often, this can lay the foundation for a successful relationship more than camaraderie and common interests. If you are a little anxious, take a deep breath and try to relax. Realize that becoming acquainted is a critical step that will lead to even bigger positive results.

C *ase* S *tudy*

WORLD BANK

Begun in 1997 by World Bank to provide increased opportunities for women in its Asian offices, its mentoring program has grown to over 16 mentoring programs. The company now has a database to keep track of managers and employees who have agreed to act as mentors.

Each of the World Bank programs has its own coordinator, and these coordinators—all of whom have full-time jobs in the bank—meet every two months to discuss progress. Coordinators are expected to have good interpersonal skills and not only commitment to the mentoring effort but also to the bank itself—they must be willing to stay with the bank for five years. Mentors are allowed two mentees.

Each mentoring group has a steering committee of six to eight employees who match mentors to employees and otherwise oversee the program activities. Training is provided for both mentors and mentees. In pairing mentors and protégés, the mentoring committees check to see that no reporting relationship exists, and that there is at least one grade level that separates mentors from mentees. An effort is made to match cultural similarities and educational levels, like pairing a Ph.D. to an employee with a doctorate.

The program is a facilitated mentoring effort but there are no guidelines regarding the number of meetings between mentor and mentee or the duration of the mentorship. Sessions between mentors and mentees are intended to provide feedback about their effort to achieve their career goals.

After two months, mentoring partners are asked if they are meeting and how the mentoring process is working. There is not only oral feedback but written evaluations that focus on the pairs' progress in career planning and development. A third evaluation is used to get feedback from the pair on the mentorship level achieved.

An outside consulting firm is also used to do a final evaluation, to measure the return from the partnerships.

The program includes an exit strategy for mentoring relationships that go awry. The World Bank is pleased with the results to date. Mentees report that the mentoring relationships have raised their morale, increased their capabilities, and contributed to greater career progress. Mentors have said that they have become better listeners and stimulated greater interest in coaching their own staff.

To keep the program momentum live, mentors gather at monthly breakfast meetings or wine and cheese parties, or even go bowling. The company also stages mentor recognition events and program relaunches. Regional vice presidents send thank you e-mails to those serving as mentors.

3

BEING A ROLE MODEL, BROKER, AND ADVOCATE

While most of the attention associated with mentoring focuses on coaching, there are three other responsibilities of mentors: role model, broker or link to others, and advocate or cheerleader. Let's look at these three roles in depth.

ROLE MODEL

A role model is a person so effective or inspiring in some professional or personal way that he or she is a model for others. When the role model is also the individual's mentor, he or she is someone whom the protégé admires or looks up to, a person the protégé would like to emulate. The mentor has reached a level of accomplishment in a role that the protégé aspires to with qualities and attributes that the mentee wishes to acquire.

Sharon, a protégé for a mentor who oversees work on a plant shop floor, adds this about mentors as role models: "Mentors should be role models, but role models who haven't forgotten where they came from, how they got to where they are now, and are always looking back to see if they can help those that came from the very same place." She adds, "I think a good mentor encourages me to believe I can get to where he is."

When people assume the role of mentor, they know that they will be role models, whether they like it or not. It will be their behavior that people will watch and emulate. It is their leadership qualities that others will study and want to duplicate. It is even the smile that they give staff members that people will want to copy.

This puts tremendous pressure on you as a mentor to be a good role model. As a mentor, you want to set a good example, not behave in a manner that represents a horrible warning. You want to be worthy of emulation—at least, most of the time. Toward that, keep this thought in mind: *You will always be on stage.* No matter where you are or what you are doing, it is bound to get back to your protégé and influence his or her behavior.

Your mentees will hear about how you interacted with someone or how confident you seemed in a specific situation. You can never fully relax in the workplace—you are always a mentor, and your behaviors will be assessed by the person whom you are mentoring.

For instance, whatever the task you have to do, you want to be sure that you are well prepared to handle the work. That's the message you want to send to your protégés. If you give the impression that you believe you can just wing things, then, your protégé is likely to figure that's all right—and he or she will do it too.

Of course, not everything will go as expected—there will even be days when nothing goes well. Your protégé will watch to see how you behave in the face of problems. This is not the time to lose your temper or seem out of control. It is the time to seem prepared even if you aren't, smile, and get through the situation. In other words, don't let your protégé see you sweat.

Assuming that you practice the values you preach, your protégés are likely to practice these values too. When you mentor employees within your organization, and your values reflect the strategic mission of your organization, you can expect the support of your protégés in achieving these missions. Certainly, they will be more alert to opportunities for achieving them and more willing to extend themselves to accomplish corporate strategies. Research shows that managers who say they have role models in their organizations are more committed to their organization's values and goals. As a role model, you provide not only insight into the skills and behaviors individuals need to learn to become more effective performers, but also an inspirational aspect—you motivate your employees and managers to give their all to achieve the same objectives as you hold for your organization.

When your protégé expresses a desire to build his or her leadership talents, then you need to take time with the individual to further spark that desire. Ask your protégé how you can help—and then be quiet and listen to learn more about your protégé's desires and then follow through by providing opportunities to help achieve those goals. In a similar situation, you can expect your mentee to do the same.

As a role model, your behavior itself will influence your protégé. If someone were to take a video of your behavior over a day, would you be proud of your behavior or, like some of the losers on the popular television show *The Apprentice* as they behold the example they set as prospective leaders, cringe in embarrassment.

What kinds of traits and characteristics should you be exhibiting that you would be proud for your protégé to emulate?

- *Integrity.* Do you act in ways that are ethical, earning the respect and trust of your mentees and others with whom you do business? In other words, are you walking the talk—that is, doing more than giving lip service to the ideals we all should be living up to? In a survey reported in *Fast Company* magazine in 1997, 93 percent of 40,000 people surveyed admitted to lying regularly and habitually in the workplace. Are you really an exception?
- *Consideration of others' feelings.* You should be expressing your own feelings and convictions with courage but your remarks should be balanced with consideration for the feelings and convictions of others.
- *Promise keeping, not just promise making.* Based on your past actions, have you demonstrated that your word can be trusted? Keep in mind that your credible reputation can be lost if you veer from the truth—even if the reason seems "good," like not wanting to discourage someone who is looking soon to a promotion or losing the support of someone whose help you need to complete a project by a specific date. Whatever the reason, your credibility will suffer.
- *Authenticity.* Here, I'm talking about the ability to put aside false appearances and truly be ourselves. This isn't so easy today. Rather than be themselves, many people have developed the art of *appearing* to be themselves, which doesn't fool people for long. Not only is authenticity a value you want your protégés to emulate, it is one that you truly need yourself as a leader if you are to achieve strong relationships in your work. You don't need to share highly personal information but you want to demonstrate both an interest in your associates' lives outside of the work environment and a willingness to share information about your family and friends—even your dog.
- *Honoring confidentiality.* In particular, your protégé will be looking for evidence that you can be trusted not to reveal information told in confidence. If you promise to keep some knowledge secret, then you should honor that promise. Although all personal and sensitive infor-

mation should be treated as confidential, if you are still in doubt, ask. It is better to get clarification with the person who shared the information with you than to take liberties and make the wrong assumption.

- *Standing and delivering bad news.* No one wants to be the bearer of bad tidings, but the ability to do it well—which requires considerable foresight—is also a worthy value. There will be times when you have bad news you can't divulge, for example when the possibility of downsizing is undecided. But let's assume that you are asked if there is a downsizing coming. Better to acknowledge that it is being considered but nothing is yet final than to deny the rumor entirely.

This value list could be endless. Take out a sheet of paper and draw a line down the middle. On one side, list those values that you have. On the other side, list those values that you need to develop or fine-tune for the future, particularly if they will contribute to the respect with which others will hold you and make you a better example for others to emulate.

I saw a list of four questions each of us should ask ourselves at the end of the day.

1. What impact have my actions had on achieving my company's goals?
2. What impact have my actions had on my own career?
3. What did I learn today from my own actions?
4. How will I do better tomorrow?

Let me add a fifth question: What impact have my actions had on others—in particular, my protégé or mentee if I have one? As a mentor, that is a critical addition to the list.

BROKER

Your protégé may not have the contacts you do, and as a mentor, your role is to make them available.

You have listened to your protégé's career goals and you have served as a sounding board for her ideas. Now you have to draw on favors owed to you by colleagues and other professional contacts to get the additional information or resources that your protégé needs to make her plans work. You act almost as a corporate uncle or aunt for the mentee, clearing the path for her to reach those whose approval is needed for the ideas to be tried.

But to serve as a broker for your protégé, you have to have solid contacts. That means that you have to be skilled in building a network of individuals to whom you can go to help your mentee.

If you looked at your Rolodex, would you feel confident that you could help your protégé, or do you need to strengthen your contacts within and outside your company and industry before you can truly help your protégé?

What will that entail?

Your first step is to make a commitment to build your network. Not only will that help your protégé but it will also help you in your career. After that, there are some techniques that will help you increase your contacts both within and outside your company.

Develop a 25-second infomercial about yourself. Be prepared to introduce yourself and to answer the question, "What do you do?" in 25 seconds or less in a clear, concise, and memorable way. Remember, first impressions count, and you have a limited time to make a good impression. Don't just give your job title; tell the other party what you do. You may be vice president of sales for XYZ Tools but don't just say that. Let the other person know what that entails: "I develop winning marketing campaigns for my firm." Or, let's say that you run a training and development company. You might tell the group, "I create top performers for *Fortune* 500 companies."

Do your research. Know more about the people you will be meeting and their interests. Articles about these people in either print or electronic versions of industry, association, and trade magazines and newsletters will present information that you can use to start a conversation with someone. This will enable you to plan in advance how to enter into conversations with the individuals you will be meeting for the first time at a gathering. For instance, you might ask someone, "What brought you to this meeting?" Another good opening line might be, "What business are you in?" or, "How useful do you find these meetings to be?" Still another question might be, "This is my first meeting. How does this compare to others you've attended?"

Did you notice that each of these questions is open-ended; that is, they require more than a one-word answer? The trick is to get the other person talking and to start a conversation—to break the ice.

Introduce yourself to the speaker. Tell him or her how much you are looking forward to the talk and mention something specific about the topic or speaker. You will be able to do this because you have prepared in advance.

After the presentation, follow up by sending a note saying how much you enjoyed the talk and mentioning a helpful piece of information you took away.

Add the individual's business card to your Rolodex, and indicate when you met and details about your conversation. If you come upon some information that might help the individual, contact him or her and share your news. Before you know it, you will be meeting regularly with the person because now he or she is a member of your network, willing to help you when the need arises.

Have a list of "get to know you" questions. The focus here is on the person with whom you are speaking. Depending on the circumstances, here are some questions with which you can start your list: Why did you come to this session? Where do you work and what do you do? What other sessions have you attended? What do you do when you aren't working? What do you love about your job? What types of projects do you get involved in? What have you done recently?

After you've introduced yourself, transfer the focus from yourself to the other person. Because people love to talk about themselves, this should sustain the conversation for as long as you wish.

Set a goal for every event you attend. You might try to make a set number of quality connections and then commit yourself to contact the individuals afterward, or even set up a follow-up meeting over lunch. At the very least, you should send a short "thank you for your time and conversation" note to the people you met.

Even more important, you should have a goal for your networking effort. Ask yourself: What opportunities do I want my networking to offer? Is it a position in senior management? Maybe you have begun to think about what you will do after you retire, or you have an idea for a new line of products or services for your organization and you need more information. Such broader goals will help you select the events you choose to attend at which to network.

Act like the host, not like a guest. Even if it isn't your meeting, go out of your way to make others comfortable. You will be remembered after the event, and will be in a position later on to call for a helping hand for yourself or your protégé.

Listen carefully with a bias toward action. What do people need that you can offer? Always be ready to give information, resources, or help to others. If someone says, "I'm ready for a vacation!" answer by saying, "I have a terrific travel agent. Would you like her name?" If they mention a work problem and you know someone who had a similar problem and found a solution, offer to bring the two together. Put aside thoughts about your phone calls at the office (and don't forget to turn off your cell phone), and pay attention to the here and now and the needs of those around you.

Demonstrate that you can be trusted. For individuals you meet to remain a permanent part of your network, you need to demonstrate to them that you are reliable. If they ask you for something by a certain time, meet the deadline. Don't take advantage of their kindness—respect their time. If you promise someone that you'll call her on Tuesday, do it. That's how you teach someone that you will do what you say you will do. If you promise someone that you'll provide X items for an auction, provide X-plus items. That way, you will demonstrate that you will go that extra mile for the person.

Be ready to give. Before an event or meeting with someone already in your network, have three resources, tips, or opportunities to share. Having things to give makes it easy for you to go from just associating with people to interacting and exchanging with them, which leads, in turn, to personal and professional opportunities.

Network within your organization. Never forget to increase the contacts you have nationally and internationally within your own company. Review your firm's organization chart. Do you know people at all levels of the organization? Do they know your name and what you do? Do you know all the people whose work intersects yours in any way? Are you involved in any cross-functional efforts or interdepartmental activities (temporary assignments, committees, task forces, special projects, or volunteer activities)? Do you take every opportunity to meet face to face with others about trends that will affect your job in the future and the tools to get the job done today?

The stronger your own network—particularly within the organization if you are mentoring someone also inside your organization—the more you can do as broker for your protégé.

ADVOCATE

As advocate for your protégé, you are his cheerleader, offering positive feedback to him about his work to ensure he is given the chance to test his wings. You recommend that your mentee is chosen to head corporate projects and otherwise give him the opportunity to advance professionally. If the protégé has a desire to set up his own business, you help the individual find the venture capitalists to finance the project, assuming that you think his business idea is sound.

Can Your Opinion Be Trusted?

As such, you have to be known to others as someone whose judgment can be trusted. This means that you should not have the reputation as someone who goes around praising everyone you come in contact with, using grandiose terminology without reason. Such individuals are known to tell their staff members that they are doing the greatest work imaginable, and that they are the best staff ever. They tell their own manager that he or she is the best supervisor since the creation of bosses. Customers are told that their children are the brightest, the best athletes, the best looking, and so forth.

In writing up performance assessments, these executives and managers write glowing performance reviews, inferring that everyone on their staff walks on water. They tend to overlook or minimize problems and laugh off shortcomings.

To these managers, the world seems perfect—and those they mentor are, likewise, perfect. So, needless to say, prospective protégés, at first, would relish the chance to have such an individual mentor them. It would be fun, their egos would rise, and likely it would be less trying than their relationship with their own supervisor for whom they are continually stretching themselves professionally to satisfy. But once someone becomes a protégé of an exaggerating congratulator, they come to realize that their new mentor isn't really very helpful. As you will discover in Chapter 4, "Mentor as Career Counselor," they will come to discount exaggerated praise and lip service and lose respect and confidence in the mentor. They eventually will view the mentor's comments as a joke if all that is given is praise.

More important, your reputation as someone who gives praise without reason will make it almost impossible for you to help a protégé, even someone who truly has the capabilities you credit the protégé with. Everyone soon picks up on your exaggerations about those with whom you work. This will backfire not only on you but also on your protégé. Your feedback won't be respected by those whose help your protégé needs, and your protégé will neither learn under your mentorship nor get opportunities from others.

Why do some managers give praise whether it has been earned or not? Some executives and managers feel that their supervisory responsibility includes acting as public relations representative for their team. They believe that as long as the group seems happy, the organization will believe that the department or division is running smoothly. Some managers don't want to confront a problem in performance and consequently prefer to be blind to its existence. This behavior carries over to their relationship with their protégé.

If you want to perform your role as advocate, you need to have a reputation for giving praise that is genuine and sincere. When you speak to others about your protégé, you have to be specific, not talk in generalities. Be prepared to cite specific instances in which your protégé demonstrated potential.

Choosing Your Medium

In your role as advocate, you will be communicating to others in writing, telephone conversations, and face-to-face conversations. With written communications, you'll have plenty of time to choose your words carefully. On the telephone, the person on the phone will hear your words and experience the tone of your voice and inflexion. In face-to-face interactions, the other party will be able to judge your body language and facial expression, in addition to hearing your words, tone of voice, and inflexion. For face-to-face communications to be effective there must be agreement among the style of communication (the inflexion and tone of voice), the substance of your communication—that is, the words—and the silent communications (the body language and facial expressions).

So, being an advocate isn't as simple as it seems. For instance, if you put your recommendation in writing, keep in mind that it will be a lasting document, one that many people other than the individual to whom you sent the letter will see. So you want to be sure that this permanent document reflects well on you, as well as on your protégé.

If you have some reservations and yet believe that your protégé deserves a chance to test her skills, you may prefer to phone in your recommendation, with praise about the mentee. If you believe that a personal conversation will help you to make your case, you may want to use the phone to set up a time to meet with this third party to talk face to face about your protégé.

Communicating Face to Face

When talking to this individual about your protégé, you may want to "sell" your comments by speaking in a manner that will enhance acceptance of your remarks. For instance, some individuals may be interested in only the big picture. What did your protégé do that is relevant to his or her need? Once they hear that the person is skilled at leading IT projects or getting a new product to market on time, they will be satisfied and ready to decide whether the individual can help him or her. No further details are needed and would only muddy the discussion. On the other hand, there are people who are very detail-oriented. They want to know the specifics. If you are selling your protégé to one of these individuals, you need to be prepared to fully paint the picture for them—from A to Z. What specifically did he do? How long did it take her to complete the work? How was his relationship with others on the project?

Beyond these characteristics, you should also consider how the individual with whom you will be meeting views the world.

Each of us has a preference for how we perceive the world. The specific means is evident by the words we use. Likewise, when we meet with someone, we are more likely to convince him or her by our own verbiage. For example, some people are more visually oriented—they "see" the world and communicate accordingly. For instance, they might say, "I see what you mean," or "I can picture what he did." So, you would be more persuasive if you told such an individual, "Imagine this: Here's Tim, with only two days to finish the proposal, and no one to help. He stayed late into the night, working on the document, a cup of coffee his only refreshment, to complete the work on schedule."

Do you see the picture? So will the individual whose help Tim now needs.

Other individuals with whom you will work may be more focused on what they hear. So they will use auditory words in their discussions. They may say, "That response was clear as a bell" or "Your idea of including him sounds great." In turn, you might want to tell them how "Tim is very clear about his goals and very persuasive in gaining others' support" or "Tim is well versed in the ins and outs of risk management and can hold his own in team discussions."

Still other individuals talk in terms of emotion. To them, "feeling" that someone performed well is important. To gain their support for Tim, you have to talk to them in their own language. You might tell them how "Tim is sensitive to the needs of customers" or "Tim is always concerned that team members get the credit they have earned when he heads up a team."

The Unspoken Words

Even when you choose your words carefully, there is still the possibility that your recommendation or advocacy of your protégé will fail because of problems with the way you gave your praise. The inflexion and intonation can be at odds with your words. Keep in mind that nonverbal communication influences almost 90 percent whether a message gets through as sent.

Consider the following statement: "Mary did a dynamite job on her presentation to the organization this week." Sounds great, right? But let's assume that you are talking to one of those individuals who needs much more detail. Further, as you say the words, you inadvertently emphasize the words "this week." As you answer questions from the other party whose support Mary needs to move upward in the organization, you also avoid eye contact. Maybe you are looking at your watch or tapping your pencil on the table, suggesting you are uncomfortable during the conversation. Whether intentional or not, you are sending a negative message about your protégé to someone critical to her future.

So you can see how responsibilities as role model, broker, and advocate are as important—sometimes, even more important—to your protégé as your role as coach.

R e l a t i o n s h i p   B u i l d i n g

It will be evident as you read this book, that mentoring within an organization actually occurs at three levels—the individual, the group/team, and the organization/culture.

1. *Individual mentoring.* As a mentor to an individual, your most significant contribution may be to identify the preferred behaviors and model them.
2. *Team mentoring.* In team settings, as a mentor (either team leader or sponsor), your role will be to form your team, work with it to set goals, ensure team members have the needed skills, and manage the group through accomplishment of its objectives. Finally, upon completion of the project, you will participate in the celebration of its success. As a mentor, however, your key role may be as broker, ensuring that your team has the resources that it will need to accomplish its objective.
3. *Organization mentoring.* Here, your role will be to work to create a culture that will support mentoring efforts—not only formal but informal. For mentoring to occur throughout your organization, those within must care for the people they work with. The organization itself should be concerned about the growth and development of everyone within.

C a s e S t u d y

MENTORSHIP OVERSEAS

At Spangdahlem Air Base in Germany, middle school students are matched with U.S. Air Force mentors who help them with their studies. The goal is to build student self-esteem and bolster academic performance. The volunteers spend one hour per week with the students helping them with their reading, math, and science assignments.

A teacher at the school is mentorship coordinator. Teachers and parents nominate students for the mentorship program. Once a student's parents give permission, a mentor volunteer is matched with a student.

Students with mentors complete a survey to determine their interests. The mentors are also asked which grade level they prefer and what their strengths are, and then are matched with students they can help the most.

4

MENTOR AS
CAREER COUNSELOR

The most fortunate of mentors are those whose protégés fall into the category of high potential; that is, these are individuals that, with minimal coaching, have the ability to move up in their current organization or found and build a business of their own. A study done by Spencer Stuart, reported in *The 5 Patterns of Extraordinary Careers,* identified the characteristics of those managers and employees most likely to succeed.

HIGH-POTENTIAL MENTEES

Authors Richard A. Smith and James M. Citrin, both of Spencer Stuart, describe as high potentials those who: are curious and proactive in their quest for knowledge; practice open, honest communication; do their defined jobs well but also are creative, working hard to make their ideas a reality; focus on both short-term and long-term goals; and demonstrate an eagerness to accomplish more than the duties outlined in their job description. Ideally, these are the individuals you would want to recruit and work beside. Certainly, for less experienced individuals, they would make outstanding mentors. And for those executives and managers looking to nurture a talented manager or staff member, they would make outstanding mentees.

As a mentor, imagine how you could help individuals, already with such talents, advance in their careers. Your task would be to provide minimum advice and maximum kudos.

Unfortunately, most candidates for mentoring aren't so perfect. With help from you, however, they can overcome shortcomings and offer the promise of the previously described high-potential managers and employees.

We're talking about how, as a mentor, you can counsel other executives, managers, and staff to help them advance in their careers. To do this, you will perform your responsibilities as role model, broker, advocate, and cheerleader. But mentoring specifically to help someone advance in their careers also demands a clear understanding of the individual's desires for the future.

THE FIRST STEP

Before you have a clear idea of the individual's goals, your mentee must be clear about his objectives. Strangely enough, many of us want to advance in our careers but we're not so sure what that means in real terms. In other words, what would we like to be doing in the next two years, five years, or ten years from now? How about our firm? Would we want to move up the chain of command in our organization or do our career goals demand that we consider a change in employer?

These are the first questions that you, as a mentor, need to address with your mentee. At the very least, you should ask your mentee to make a list and put in order of importance how you can help her move to the next level. Sometimes, you may be surprised to discover that your mentee, as talented and conscientious as you expected, also lacks self-confidence.

There are countless fears, and many of them show up at work. While you won't find your mentee running and hiding under his desk, you might find other signs—like isolation or hostility when you talk about career advancement. Rather than face the fear of failure or rejection if he made an effort to advance, your mentee may tell you that he is quite content where he is in the organization.

Part of your mentoring responsibility may be to make your mentee aware of his capabilities and encourage her to take the risk that comes with making an effort to gain the attention of those who make the promotion decisions. Your task may be to talk your mentee out of the belief that the nose-to-the-grindstone approach will reap its own rewards. What will reap rewards is projecting a positive image of one's self to get people to know and recognize you, your strengths, and your potential. As mentor, your task is to help your mentee with this.

What will this entail? The first step as a mentor is to encourage your mentee to discard that outmoded image of herself, as well as discard any outmoded habits. If your mentee is reluctant to imagine a better position than the one she currently has, it may be important to help her create a more satisfying new vision of herself. At a subconscious level, encourage her to see herself receiving a promotion and diving successfully into the new job.

I know one mentor who is a trainer. She's taken under her wing a consultant who is also interested in being a trainer. Mildred is well aware that her mentee lacks self-confidence, and she goes out of her way to make her realize how she admired the qualities her mentee possesses. When they are together, and Mildred introduces her mentee to others, she expands on her introduction of her protégé. It's done not only for those to whom she's introducing her mentee but for her mentee. Each time, Mildred plays up her mentee's past achievements. Eventually, Mildred hopes her mentee will appreciate her own capabilities and be more self-confident. Mildred tells me that she doesn't slump so much, which is one way we communicate our insecurity. So Mildred's mentee may be on her way to changing her self-image.

As a mentor, you need to encourage your mentee to put aside any fears he or she may have of failing in that position on which you both are focused. Acknowledge that there will be some stresses associated with the promotion, but point out as well that there will be exciting opportunities associated with success.

CAREER ASPIRATIONS

Because some mentees can get stuck in positions, they may need to be prodded to think in new ways. If your mentee isn't clear about the next career step, ask her those things she really enjoys doing; that is, what tasks truly make her happy. Maybe your mentee can remember one or two moments in the near past that were especially satisfying. When you meet with your mentee, you want her to talk about these. As you question your mentee, you should get insights into your mentee's thinking about the next rung on the career ladder. Not only do you want to know if your mentee believes that she is qualified to climb that rung but also what that rung is in your mentee's mind.

If you work in the same organization as your mentee, you are best qualified to judge how realistic the mentee's goal is. If you are not colleagues, but you are familiar with your mentee's company and/or industry, then you may be able to assess how realistic your mentee's plan for advancement is. Is the organization growing so there is room for your mentee to rise in the organization or is the company currently held back by the economy or state of the industry? If you are mentoring a colleague, you may not want to discourage him if you see no opportunity for promotion at this time. On the other hand, you need to be honest with your mentee. If now is not the time to shoot for that ideal position he wants, you may suggest that your mentee seek a promotion that would position him for consideration at a later time, and maybe even offer the opportunity to better qualify for that opportunity when it becomes available, even if it entails zigzagging across the managerial ranks.

Some mentees are reluctant to consider an alternative to their ideal job, but zigzagging within the ranks is an option that should not be ignored, particularly in tough economic times when companies are running lean with little opportunity for promotion. Sometimes, it will help if you send them out to do research about available positions and the requirements. Laura had wanted to move up to assistant marketing manager yet lacked some critical skills for the position. Her mentor knew that and realized that Laura needed to make a commitment to some on-the-job training, maybe even a semester at a community college, to qualify for the position. He suggested her need for training, but she was resistant. Rather than fight over the matter, he suggested she have a heart-to-heart talk with both the head of marketing and the human resources manager to get a clear idea of the qualifications for the position.

Laura came back with a much more realistic view. While she still was enthusiastic about her career goal, she realized it would take longer—and would require some extra training—and accepted her mentor's advice.

WRITING A VISION STATEMENT

With a realistic picture of the organization chart before you, opportunities for openings based on strategic and succession plans, and the strengths and weaknesses of your mentee, you both should sit down and prepare a vision statement. Comparable to the kind of statement corporations prepare that align mission and strategy, your mentee's vision statement should align the next position (think vision or mission statement) with the mentee's development plans (which would be comparable to the company's strategic plans).

In developing this document, you want to be as specific as possible. Remember, how in corporate planning, we develop SMART objectives; that is, specific, measurable, achievable, realistic, and timely (scheduled) goals. Likewise, the development goals that you and your mentee should set should be SMART.

The development goals should be detailed, particular, or focused. That is, they should clearly state what is to be achieved and how that will be done. The action steps that you and your mentee plan to take to position the mentee for the next career move should be quantifiable. Beyond that, however, they should be important to those who are responsible for making the promotion.

Let me share with you a story here.

HARD WORK ISN'T ALWAYS ENOUGH

Jasmine, a young and talented editor, had been hired to produce her organization's internal newsletter. A year afterward, she was also given responsibility for the firm's intranet and several of the pages on its Web site. Her initiative and hard work had gained her the attention of one of the senior managers, Sam, and he had chosen to help her with her career.

It was very clear to Sam how dedicated Jasmine was. Many weekends, Jasmine left her young daughter with her husband so she could work at the office to assist on other writing assignments. Her goal and that of Sam was for her to become head of the Web publishing group. Both believed that senior management would be impressed with Jasmine's conscientiousness and reward her accordingly. Part of the plan was her request to produce a special issue of the internal newsletter to celebrate the company's twenty-fifth anniversary. Feedback was positive and substantial. Jasmine and her mentor, Sam, felt that she was a shoe-in for a promotion. Not so.

The head of the Web publishing unit position went to a colleague who had raised sales off the Web by 10 percent. No, this individual didn't put in long hours at work, come up with great looking pages for the site, or add new content to the Web. Karl had done some research and identified several new search engines that would draw potential customers to the firm's site. Which is what interested senior management.

Jasmine got an excellent performance review—from Karl—but putting out more issues of the internal newsletter and a better looking intranet and Web site wasn't viewed as important as that 10 percent increase in customer sales on the Web that Karl brought the organization.

Not only must the goals be measurable but they must reflect the needs of the organization. It's one of the reasons why you, as a colleague, make an excellent mentor—you bring to your role knowledge about what's important to senior management so you can direct your mentee to those efforts that will gain attention and hopefully lead to promotion.

Needless to say, the development goals you and your mentee set should be achievable. Unlike the goals that a mentee might set with his or her manager, they need not be in writing. Further, they should not be shared with others—they should be kept between you and your mentee.

Just as the career plan should be realistic, so, too, should the goals. While Jasmine and Sam's plan didn't work, both Jasmine and Sam had given serious thought to the cost of an extra, expanded issue of the internal newsletter and improved intranet site before they agreed that Jasmine should use those opportunities to demonstrate more fully to management her employability.

Needless to say, because Sam and Jasmine had some idea when the position she wanted would be available, they knew that Jasmine had to complete the extra newsletter and redesign of the intranet in time to impact the appointment.

Sam and Jasmine's SMART development plan didn't get her the appointment she wanted, but it did give her greater visibility which might have explained how six months later she was given responsibility for a second newsletter, this one for the firm's customers. More money and an upgrade went with the position.

PUT IT IN PENCIL

Mentors with whom I've talked suggest that the development plan, as well as the vision or career statement, should be written but in pencil. Visualizing the future is hard enough—just try putting your own dreams on paper—but times and situations change, and the development plan will need to be adapted accordingly. While you want your mentee's dream to be something within reach, that doesn't mean that your mentee can't dream big. You can address the feasibility of the development plan and career goal later.

Determination of the individual's goals and plans to achieve these goals demand you put on your coaching hat as mentor. For one, you will need to assess your mentee's strengths and weaknesses and share your views with that mentee. You need to consider not only the individual's skills, abilities, and knowledge but also attitude.

ATTITUDINAL PROBLEMS

At the beginning of this chapter, I identified five positive traits that define a high-potential candidate for advancement. Here are some less attractive qualities that you may find in your mentees.

Selfishness

Your mentee may be focused only on what he wants and may have little interest in the needs and wants of others. Your mentee may operate by the old adage: If I don't look out for number one, then who will? You may recognize peers from this description—those with a bad case of I-tis: What do I want? How can I get it? Why didn't I get the promotion? While this attention to self seems to be a part of today's materialistic culture, actually it's been around for many years.

The story goes that back in 1864, a member of Abraham Lincoln's cabinet died suddenly. There was a furious scramble for the vacant post. One potential candidate quickly rushed into Lincoln's office and asked, "I've always wanted that position. Can I take his place right now?" to which Lincoln calmly replied, "Certainly, if the undertaker doesn't mind."

Should you find yourself with a protégé very focused on herself, then part of your responsibility will be to get the individual to look beyond her desires and help others get what they want. Your intent should be to show the candidate how reciprocity can work to her benefit—that is, how a helping hand is often returned in kind.

Interpersonal Conflict

We're really talking about conflicts that arise from differences in opinion and competition for opportunities for recognition and visibility. Such battles are inevitable in every organization, but some battles turn into major warfare. There are managers whose behavior makes collegial relationships difficult, if not impossible, impeding innovation and productivity.

Poor Communication

Maybe the individual uses the wrong word or the wrong tone of voice or his body sends a different message than the mouth dispenses. Another problem: lack of listening. The manager says he hears what he is told but the truth is he really isn't listening. He just wants to talk and talk and talk. Often, this person is closed to any other individual's ideas but his own.

Too Emotional

You might find yourself with a protégé with a tendency to shoot herself in the foot, guilty of frequent stupid outbursts or ridiculous acts. Failure to keep emotions under control can cost a very talented worker opportunity for advancement, and sometimes the individual isn't even aware that the problem exists. Should you have a protégé suffering from a number of hot buttons, your role is to teach her how to keep emotions under control.

Jealousy

Your protégé comes to you upset because he just learned that he won't get the promotion he felt he had earned. He wants to quit, and your task is to convince him that there will be other opportunities for advancement—maybe, this wasn't even the right one for him.

When Jeff was passed over for promotion, he expected his mentor Phil to step in and defend his right to get the promotion. He was disappointed when Phil, instead, suggested that Jeff calm down and think about the job he had missed out on. Yes, it was the next natural step up, but was it what he wanted? Jeff was a salesman and he had to admit that he enjoyed meeting prospects, building relationships with customers, and closing sales. The position of sales manager entailed filing reports, keeping pace with demands from headquarters, and spending time in the office. Sales management wasn't his cup of tea. He and Phil needed to sit down and rethink the career management plan to direct his future career based on what he truly liked to do.

TEACHING AN INTROVERT TO NETWORK

In this book, I've pointed to your role as broker and how important it is to have a strong network of contacts to support your protégé's career aspirations. But your mentee should not be dependent on you for all the contacts she will need. So you will need to spend time sharing your networking skills with your protégé as part of your career counseling tasks.

For some individuals, this will be easier than with others. Some individuals are extroverts and take naturally to networking whereas others are introverts and are less comfortable walking up to strangers and beginning a conversation. If your protégé falls into the latter category, that person can still be a good networker. As the individual's mentor, you need to point out how she can build her own network if she uses her introverted nature to her advantage.

For instance, most introverts are good listeners. Ironically, while they let others do the talking, these individuals consider them to be brilliant conversationalists—people like to talk. Because they are thoughtful and reflective—positive traits—they are trusted. Those who know them are willing to lend them a hand when they need a favor.

Mike is a friend of mine. He is always ready with praise and appreciation for others. When he says something, he has thought carefully before speaking. He is constantly thinking of others. He gives freely of his expertise and advice in his profession as a trainer and is an active volunteer at a local community club. He doesn't consider himself a particularly social person, yet he has many loyal friends who would, and have, helped him out whenever he needed a favor.

Mike may not relish the idea of walking up to a stranger and starting a conversation, but when you get him to talk about training disadvantaged children, a subject he is passionate about, his shyness magically disappears.

With the help of a colleague who is now Mike's mentor, Mike has learned how to transfer that same passion when he is talking to prospective clients about the impact training can have on employees' performance. He is able now to speak with enthusiasm and conviction about the impact he has had on other work teams.

Mike learned how to build his loyal network and also participate in his mentor's network by taking the following baby steps:

1. *Set a goal.* His goals don't involve as much stretch but over time the results have become evident by the ever-increasing business his small firm is enjoying. Specifically, Mike and his mentor agreed that once a week Mike would go through his contact list and call three people just to say hello. These brief calls have been effective, each leading to an immediate job or to a new client.

2. *Begin with a compliment.* This is an easy and effective way to start a conversation. After all, everyone likes to get a compliment.

3. *Use a script.* Mike and his mentor have actually developed a short yet detailed script to use. It's designed to help him introduce himself to strangers. He's rehearsed it so he comes across naturally. He also has learned about the importance of researching any firm he plans to contact. It has become second nature to him, and enables him to get past the administrative assistant or assistant manager and ultimately talk to the training manager. He and his mentor even have put together a script to get him over the first few minutes of a face-to-face meeting with the person who will decide to hire Mike or not. It's a 30-second infomercial polished and rehearsed along with three "small talk" topics—current events, new movies or books, or industry news—that gets Mike past the awkwardness of the introductions.

4. *Work on eye contact.* This was tough for Mike because he is very shy. His mentor noticed from their first meeting that Mike, while a thoughtful and caring person, didn't seem to be listening or giving him his full attention when they were together. Mike always seemed to be looking elsewhere when his mentor was talking. Mike denied he was doing it when it was first brought to his attention. It turned out that he wasn't aware he was doing it. So, don't laugh, Mike's mentor got a

small bell and when he saw Mike's eyes focusing everywhere but on him, he would ring the bell. After hearing the bell about ten times in 30 minutes, Mike told me, it was hard to disagree with his mentor. Mike's mentor tells me that Mike no longer has a problem. He looks people right in the eyes. His confidence has grown and it has helped his business.

5. *Do your networking when your energy level is at the highest point of the day.* Mike is a morning person, so he tries to set up his business meetings for the first thing in the morning. When the meeting is scheduled for later in the day, he takes a quick "power nap" to energize himself. If you have ever talked to an introvert, you will discover that they tire from long social engagements; consequently, they are the first to leave parties or will be found seated by themselves or quietly talking with one other person on the sidelines. Mike has learned not only to charge himself up to be alert and ready for opportunities to make contacts but also to use his propensity for sitting quietly alone to meet and "really get to know others." Many of the quiet times that he has spent with others at social events have led to business contacts and ultimately new business for his firm.

His mentor is proud of how Mike has overcome his introversion that makes him extremely sensitive to his classroom of students but initially uncomfortable hustling for new business clients. How did Mike's mentor discover that Mike needed help in networking? Don't laugh but he shadowed him through a business reception and observed Mike's behavior.

THE SHADOW KNOWS

Shadowing is an effective tool, and it works two ways. As a mentor, you can invite your mentee to a meeting or another situation where she can watch you and other executives and managers within the organization at work. After the fact, you can sit down with your mentee and discuss what happened, identifying behavior to which your mentee should aspire, not only yours but that of others in the room. Alternatively, you can provide an opportunity for your mentee to test her wings at which time you will be a shadow and observe her at work.

Let's say that you are offered a project to head up. Rather than take on the task, you may recommend your mentee. Not only will this give her the opportunity to show her capability but, perhaps, she has knowledge about the project that you lack and could speed the project's completion. In recommending your mentee to head up the project, you are assuming another of your mentoring responsibilities—as an advocate. If you have credibility within the organization, and are known not to offer undeserved praise, it's likely that your mentee will get the opportunity to head up the project.

Thereafter, you may want to keep an ear open to hear how the project is getting started. If you can, you may invite yourself to attend a meeting to see how your mentee is doing in leading the team. If you see a problem, don't say anything during the meeting. Wait until the session is over to share your observations. Your objective is to provide constructive feedback.

As you'll read in Chapter 5, "Straight Talk," you want to begin by pointing to those actions by your mentee that are commendable. Next, point out targets for improvement. Rather than point out mistakes, talk about new behaviors that you would like to see your mentee exhibit. State the behavior in positive terms—what to do versus what not to do—and in specific and observable terms why such behavior is critical.

Ideally, you should help your mentee become aware of her accomplishments each step of the way. When you meet together, review progress of the career plan, in particular the good behavior being exhibited. Thus, your mentee will actually be alert to her successes, which will build self-confidence.

Toward that, you might also want to describe what you observe as a mentor about your mentee's behavior and encourage your mentee to come up with a solution herself. Rather than solve your mentee's problems for her, encourage her to identify the solution. Yes, you should work with your mentee to map out a course of action for improvement where a behavioral problem exists, but you should wait until your mentee has thought through the situation and made an effort to find her way. If you see that your mentee needs help, then you need to step in. Demonstrate that you care and try to help your mentee address the problem rather than ignore the situation or blame the mentee if it recurs.

As you counsel your mentee about advancing professionally, it's imperative that you demonstrate patient leadership. Not only are you your mentee's role model for such behavior, but it is critical to the success of the mentoring process. The initial trust and commitment between you and your mentee will remain only if you demonstrate your continued concern for your mentee and positive feelings about her career. This means that feedback throughout the development plan—indeed, any interactions between you and your mentee—must be upbeat. It must demonstrate to your mentee that you have every confidence in her ability to succeed.

S *t a r t i n g   t h e* **D** *i s c u s s i o n*

As you will discover in the next chapter, the key to your mentoring is the ability to ask questions that encourage your mentee to think. Here are some questions you can use when you first sit down with your mentee to probe about his or her career aspirations:

- As you look to your future, possibly three to five years from now, what role or occupation would you like to have and why?
- What skills, abilities, and knowledge do you need to do that job? Have you investigated this?
- What experiences would be beneficial to gain that job?
- What had you planned to do to prepare yourself for that job?
- As your mentor, what specifically can I do to support your efforts?

HELP YOUR MENTEE MARKET HIMSELF

As a mentor, you need to take on the role of teacher. If you want your mentee to succeed, you need to teach these seven tricks of successful self-marketing:

1. *Make commitments and keep those commitments.* Your mentee needs to understand that the quickest way to lose credibility is to make promises that he doesn't keep. By the way, the same applies to you as a mentor. Don't make promises to your mentee about advancement unless you can keep them. Better to underpromise—both you and your mentee.

2. *Demonstrate reliability, honesty, and respect.* Again, this is as true for you as a mentor as for your mentee. These three behaviors are essential for creating a positive image. You can't fake these behaviors—either you practice them or you do not, and if you don't, all career plans won't help you.

3. *Demonstrate initiative and optimism.* This includes a readiness to seize opportunities or convert problems into opportunities, to pursue goals beyond expectations, to influence others, and to operate from a platform of abundance and hope for success. No one considers someone who has a defeatist attitude—again, mentee or mentor—to solve problems and develop new ideas that will improve operations.

4. *Demonstrate a sincere appreciation for your colleagues.* You have to mean it when you say "thank you." Take the time and effort to show your appreciation of peers' good work.

5. *Look for opportunities to send the message that you are hard at work.* I'm not suggesting that your mentee put in late nights and long weekends—to work like a martyr—but rather your mentee should make those people who count know about his or her productivity and progress. As the individual's mentor, you also need to communicate this dedication about your mentee to those in senior management.

6. *Exhibit professionalism.* This is another of those qualities that people see when they look at a colleague. If your mentee cannot yet be described as being professional in the workplace, that should be your first objective or goal with your mentee.

7. *Use attraction.* I'm not talking about looks here. I'm talking about demonstrating a willingness to listen to others, to authentically support them, to share knowledge, and the like. Politicking works only so far. As a mentor, it is important that you make it clear to your mentee that political savvy is important but success is founded on a solid record of accomplishments and concern to help others. Otherwise, why would you be a mentor?

S a m p l e   D e v e l o p m e n t   P l a n

Career objective: Become qualified for project team leader.

Development Objective	Measure	Development Activities	Time Frame

Your mentee's development plan should specify the overall goal and each development objective. For instance, here, a development objective might be to improve project management skills, the measure might be demonstration of better leadership skills, and the means of achieving the objective might be participation on your project team or attendance at a public seminar on the fundamentals of project management, or time spent with you coaching. The dates for completion will correspond with the activities. So coaching might be continuous whereas attendance at the course might be set by the date of the program.

Action Plan for Mentee Development

You and your mentee may want to sit down and fill out a form like this. Choose skills, abilities, and knowledge critical to your protégé's advancement, rate the level of mentoring, and then develop an action plan for each competency. Ideally, identify no more than five areas for improvement each time you sit down with your mentee.

Mentoring Focus Competency	Mentoring Need (3 for high, 2 for medium, 1 for low)		
Problem Solving: Ability to identify root causes, develop action plans, and implement/follow up.	3	2	1
People Skills: Ability to motivate people from different backgrounds—demonstrates respect, caring, and fairness.	3	2	1
Customer Focus: Concern for customers—internal and external. Will go that extra mile to delight customers.	3	2	1
Teamwork: Ability to assemble, motivate, and facilitate productive activities, including meetings. Ability to get people to cooperate within and between departments.	3	2	1
Continuous Improvement: Ability to find new ways of doing things. Encourage change.	3	2	1

P *r o b l e m s   a n d*   **P** *r o b l e m*   **S** *o l v i n g*

You have been shown how mentoring can be used to boost performance or help individuals advance in their careers or make it possible for a new hire with lots of ability to hit the ground running thanks to your support. But mentoring can also be used to address management problems experienced by these same mentees, even solve a real business problem.

Your mentee may not even know that he has a serious problem in the making. All he knows is that a problem in his area of operation exists. It could be a delay in delivery of a work order, a manufacturing flaw in a product, or parts repeatedly misplaced in the warehouse. Every so often, however, your mentee has made mention of the situation. Your mentee hasn't asked for your help, hasn't even suggested that it is a serious matter; rather, he sees it as a recurring nuisance.

Is this an issue in which you should become involved? Yes, in the sense that you help your mentee see a problem in the making, help him begin to think about solving the problem, and even teach him how to use the colleagues with whom he has worked in the past to help him with the new problem. Using questions, you can help your mentee think through the problem and come to reasonable solutions.

C *a s e*   **S** *t u d y*

IT PROGRAMS AT THREE TECH FIRMS

IT talent is in such high demand that an organization can't afford to lose these employees to a competitor. Mentoring translates into long-term viability, profitability, and even shareholder value because that organization won't have to constantly replenish its staff.

Let's look at three corporate programs.

Lucent Technology. Its Information Technology Leadership Development Program is critical in identifying and developing talented IT professionals. A key element of the program is a mentoring program. Protégés are matched with senior mentors for a one-year relationship in which the mentor provides care

(continued)

or guidance. The program attracts network engineers, technical managers, and middleware developers, as well as nontechnical support staff.

The mentoring experience allows the IT employees to learn from their mentors' experiences, to be more visible within the organization, to network, and to learn about trends and resources within the company. The program also helps new hires to be assimilated more quickly into the organization. At many organizations, it falls on the shoulders of the new hires to guide themselves through the organization maze and ultimately find their own mentors, which is difficult even in small organizations but can be progressively more difficult the larger the firm. Having a formal program makes such a process much easier for new hires but it also sends a clear message from the first day to IT recruits that the company cares for their successful orientation.

The mentors at Lucent also welcome the opportunity because it gives them insights into the organization beyond their department boundaries. Not only do they get insights about other business units in the company but also learn how to be better communicators and become recognized as leaders.

Hewlett-Packard. Its eight-year-old Accelerated Development Program is a yearlong program that includes development planning, mentoring, leadership workshops, and external education. Its purpose is to groom both IT and non-IT middle managers. Hewlett-Packard spends about $35,000 for each person who goes through the program, and it enrolls at least 100 employees annually.

IBM. Its Executive Resource Program has been especially helpful to women working in IT, a male-dominated discipline for the most part. The company believes that women need positive role models in leadership positions. Underrepresented as they are in IT and also unsure of the opportunities available to them in IT, they need to believe that the company is supportive of their career advancement. This is the role of the mentoring initiative.

IBM has also created the Women of Color and Women in Technology subcommittees, the Mentoring and Employee Development Program, and the Global Women's Leadership conference, which encourage women to network and form mentoring relationships.

5

STRAIGHT TALK

There will be occasions when the role of coach is a fun one. Your responsibility is not to offer negative feedback. Rather, it is to point to positive behavior and, where self-esteem may be weak, encourage the employee or manager to appreciate his or her own capabilities.

COMMUNICATING GOOD NEWS

The process is threefold: recognize the accomplishment, say how pleased you are, and look for ways to make the capability visible to the rest of the organization.

Let's say that your protégé, Ann, is a fine writer. She is an IT technician, and has just shown you a proposal she produced for some new corporate system. You can see little you can do to make it better. Further, she has told you that she enjoyed doing the research and writing the document. After reading it through, you might tell Ann, "This is really good. I didn't know you liked to work on proposals like this one."

When she tells you how enjoyable she found the task, your next step is to determine just how much she enjoyed it: "Ann, this is really good. Is this something you'd like to do more of?"

"Yes," she says, "but my job doesn't offer very many opportunities for me to demonstrate my writing skills."

Now, you move the conversation one step further. You know that Bill, the head of purchasing, needs someone to help him submit a systems proposal to senior management. Unfamiliar with the technology he needs, he came to you for help. But based on the document before you, Ann would seem perfect for the task. "If you like this kind of work, why don't you let me tell Bill in purchasing. He needs help submitting a proposal for a new data management system. It would be a terrific opportunity for you to better understand how purchasing operates as well as influence the technology that the group ends up with. What do you say?"

Ann agrees, pleased that you not only found her proposal well done but you are willing to recommend she work with a senior manager on a similar document. This simple conversation sends a strong message to her that she matters to you and you want her to have all the opportunities to grow as professionally as possible within the organization.

POSITIVE FEEDBACK

Let's look at another coaching situation. In this instance, your role is to help a relative newcomer to your organization better understand how the company truly operates. It's one of those lessons that we really don't want to teach some bright but naïve individual who believes that talent will win. You are delighted to have Sid as your protégé and Sid is full of new and exciting ideas. During one of your meetings over lunch, however, he complains about how his ideas aren't being acted on. His own manager is a factor but he isn't placing the blame there entirely. When his boss does submit Sid's ideas to those with the authority to act on them, nothing happens. There isn't even a negative reaction from those in charge. "Am I on the wrong track?" he asks you.

You have a reputation for getting your ideas through, but it took you a long time to realize that the organization doesn't run like the policies and procedures guidelines suggest, and to learn how to overcome the obstacles within the organization. What are these obstacles?

First, there are some individuals within your organization who are risk averse and have managed to stay with the firm despite this. They accept very few new ideas—and definitely none from those outside of their own operation. Second, those who are more open to creative thinking have specific needs and tend to be blind and deaf to ideas that won't contribute to either. Finally, resources are limited, so the number-crunchers need to be fully convinced about the benefits to the organization of some operating improvement or product offering before approval is given.

None of these obstacles appears in any handbook. This is unfortunate because you have heard some of Sid's ideas, and you believe that some have tremendous potential.

As Sid's mentor, you have supported those ideas that looked workable. Now you have to go one step further and explain the realities of the organization—how he will need to build bridges to different parts of the organization to get an idea tested.

Your first step is to discuss with him how he should offer his ideas. So, you ask Sid to describe how he presents his thoughts to colleagues for follow through. "I just tell them my idea," he says. "They promise to think it over but I never hear back."

When does Sid offer his ideas? "When I come up with the idea, I tell them right off," he says. He offers a rough outline and, he admits, he isn't always explicit in describing the returns. "I just assume that they'll see why my idea makes sense," he says.

So, Sid's approach to submitting his ideas compounds the risk aversion of some managers, the silo-mentality of others, and the obsession with an issue or two of still others. This means that you not only need to coach Sid about how to present his ideas but also about how to win over one or two individuals within the organization to give serious consideration to his ideas.

This is actually a true story. Sid, the protégé in the story, now occupies the position his mentor held when the conversation took place. His mentor is now in charge of a subsidiary, and Sid is head of operations for the subsidiary. He's even a mentor himself.

Recalling the conversation, he told me how his mentor at the time helped him focus on a single idea and think it through thoroughly, particularly the investment to test the idea and subsequent return. Most important, said Sid, his mentor shared with him how he was successful in getting his ideas accepted. The ideas most likely to get attention, the mentor explained, were those that contributed to the corporate mission or strategic plan—so those were the ones he focused on. Further, said Sid, "my mentor taught me that I should set up a meeting with the individual whose feedback I'd need first to move the idea along within the organization. Don't just interrupt someone's conversation with another person to tell the individual your idea," my mentor told me. "Have the individual's full attention, and be clear about the outcome—don't just assume that the individual is smart enough to think the idea through when he or she hears it."

Sid continued, "We worked hard in perfecting my first official submission, and it went through. It saved the company almost a half-million dollars, which made it easier to get hearings for my other ideas, even from those who were risk averse. As far as the political arena went, I learned how important it was sometimes to make colleagues think one of my ideas was their own to make it happen. Those who matter will know," my mentor said, "and he was right."

In both of these instances, the feedback was constructive and focused on positive behaviors of the protégés. But part of a mentor's responsibility is also to point out shortcomings in the behavior and performance of a protégé—which is the tougher part of the responsibility.

THE OTHER SIDE OF THE COIN

None of us wants to bring a behavior problem to an employee's attention, yet as a mentor that may be your most important role. If your feedback is not constructive, then integrity will be lost, the mentee will not learn, and the relationship will suffer. You need to look beyond the momentary discomfort to see how the truth will bring greater worth to the mentoring relationship.

How you deliver your feedback is as important as what you say.

Let's look first at the impact of body language and tone of voice. For instance, you don't want a scowl on your face or, worse, a glare. Look the individual straight in the eyes. You want to appear empathetic. Your body itself should communicate honesty and openness. For instance, your protégé might think you are angry if you not only have a frown on your face but also have your arms folded in front of you. Yes, you might be simply focused on what your protégé is saying, but that may not be what your body is saying to your mentee.

Now let's consider what you say. Coaching a mentor is very different from coaching a staff member in that you have to depend on your persuasive ability to get him to see the situation from your perspective. You have no positional power to wield to demand a change in behavior. One way to convince a mentee to change either his behavior or his thinking is to focus on the impact on his career of continuing to behave or pursue that kind of thinking.

Let's assume something as simple as your protégé being repeatedly late for your lunch meetings. You don't need to get tough, threatening to walk away from the relationship. But neither should you ask angrily, "Why are you always late for our meetings?" Instead, you might say, "I'm frustrated that our meetings are not starting on time. My reason for telling you this is because I value our time together and I want us to have as much time as we can to discuss your future." In the future, your mentee isn't likely to be late—not if she realizes the importance of having access to your time to help her advance professionally. Most important, you have communicated this without letting her feel scolded. Needless to say, you can't say something like this and be late yourself for future meetings. Effective mentors walk the talk. They are role models as leaders and in everything else they say, do, and suggest. (See Chapter 3, "Being a Role Model, Broker, and Advocate.")

Behavioral problems are among those problems discussed in Chapter 7, "Mentoring through Difficult Situations." Here, I'd like to look at how you can use open, honest communication to help your mentee solve work-related problems—the way Sid did.

LEADING YOUR MENTEE

Effective mentors don't solve their mentee's problems. Rather, they guide with questions their employees through an exploration of the issues and obstacles impacting the issues, helping the protégé reach the best solution. When the mentee comes up with workable solutions or is otherwise successful, mentors need to offer positive reinforcement. They should be free with compliments and pats on the back. Effective mentors understand the value of praise—rewarding desired behaviors.

But a mentor's job doesn't start with either questions to get the mentee to think or with praise. It begins with listening. Critical to straight talk is to truly listen to your mentee's problems. How often have you wished you had someone to talk to about things that were bothering you? How many times have you experienced the relief of being able to get something off your chest just by talking it out? Providing a listening ear, without taking on the other person's problem, giving advice, or joining the "isn't it awful game," can serve as a powerful aid to your mentee. Many mentors believe that respectful listening is the premier mentoring art.

ACTIVE LISTENING

A mentor needs to hear what is troubling the mentee each time they meet. People who listen effectively are seen as more helpful, more "in tune," and tend to exert more influence over others than those who are less effective listeners. Consequently, you are more likely to win over your mentee with your viewpoint if you begin by listening to what that mentee has to say.

Barry tells me that he hears out his employees, yet his actions disprove that. When they come to him with a suggestion, for example, he politely hears their idea, and then tells them exactly what he wants them to do, without giving any consideration to their idea. I have been a coach to Barry, and I have found it almost impossible to get him to listen to my own advice on how he can improve his relationships with his staff.

One of his employees, Joe, had an appraisal and questioned several comments that Barry had placed on the appraisal. Barry told me that Joe is essential to his department and he thinks highly of him because of the support he gives the entire group, yet he declared Joe a poor team player in Joe's appraisal and accused him of taking excessive days off although Joe actually had taken far fewer days than were due him for the past year. Naturally, Joe questioned the evaluation, and even became heated because he felt it was unfair. In his anger, Joe said things about Barry that I had heard from other staff members about their supervisor. Barry was oblivious to the remarks— he never really heard them. He is unaware of the lack of respect with which he is now held by Joe and certainly is unaware that Joe, who is truly indispensable to the group, is job hunting.

Barry's problem is one common among many people. They confuse hearing with listening. Hearing is a function of biology, whereas listening is a function of intentional behavior. It is something we must choose to do. To do it effectively we need to focus our full attention on the words, body language, and meaning of the speaker. Consequently, when your mentee describes a situation or discusses with you a situation that she is troubled by, you need to focus your attention on her in a sustained manner. Allow your mentee to talk without interruptions, accepting what she is saying as genuine, at least to her, and not injecting your own views, opinions, or solutions.

ARE YOU A GOOD LISTENER?

You aren't truly listening to your mentee if:

- Your attention slips and you begin to focus on current matters in your life.
- You stop listening and begin to judge the mentee. You might focus on how wrong the mentee is or on what will impede your ability to help the mentee understand why she is wrong.
- You spend time you should be listening eagerly waiting for "your turn" to speak.
- Mentally, you rehearse your response to the mentee's description.
- You distract yourself by checking the time, making unrelated notes, or playing with your pen.
- You interrupt the mentee with a solution before she has completed her statement.

All of these will interfere with your ability to mentor your protégé because you aren't likely to fully understand the situation facing her. The last two behaviors on your part may even alienate your mentee because they tend to show that you aren't truly listening to what she is saying. Respectful listening is the ability to become absorbed in what the other person is saying about the problem, treating her words as confidential communication, not injecting your own views, opinions, or suggestions. The mentee is given the opportunity to gain insight into the problem not by having your advice but by articulating the issue—to sort things out and perhaps to develop some alternative solutions.

After your mentee has had her say, you should communicate your understanding of what she said and, if possible, what she meant. Even if you had focused your attention on your mentee's words, if you can't communicate this to her, you will be telling her that you really didn't understand—and won't reap all of the benefits of listening.

We are all familiar with the need to paraphrase to demonstrate that we are listening. First, paraphrasing means putting in your own words what you heard, not simply repeating the speaker's words. There are actually four types of paraphrasing:

1. *Restatement.* In a condensed version, you share what you heard your protégé say. Don't simply parrot her remarks—all that tells your mentee is that you listened, not that you understood what she was trying to explain.
2. *Move from the general to specific.* This assumes that your protégé was talking in generalizations. By expanding on one part of the statement or by giving an example, you demonstrate that you know where your mentee was going with her remarks.
3. *Move from the specific to the general.* This is the reverse of approach 2. Here, you paraphrase by drawing the broader picture from the remarks you heard. By doing this, you demonstrate not only that you understood the mentee's comment but also that her statement could, in fact, be generalized—maybe, have bigger implications.
4. *State in opposite terms.* Convey what your mentee said by stating the opposite. For instance, your mentee pointed out that her manager should do something. You could demonstrate your understanding by indicating what would happen if your protégé's boss didn't do as the mentee suggested.

LISTENING FOR FEELINGS

You shouldn't just listen to the message—you should also listen to the feelings. For instance, Barbara, Steve's mentee, told him, "When I made that presentation on Tuesday, I thought you'd support my position. Instead, you only sat there. You didn't open your mouth once. What's a mentor for anyway?" It should be clear what is troubling Barbara here—she's angry and she is communicating it not only by her remark but by her raised voice.

When you listen, be alert to the attitude that is being communicated. That's really what you ultimately respond to during your mentoring sessions. When your mentee shares a problem with you, very often the feeling is usually more important than the facts described. The facts are the objective reality or, at least, how the mentee sees the situation. Your mentee's feelings about the situation—whether seen as a problem or not, the dimensions of the problem, and its importance—are the issues to which you should be alert. Toward this, you want to be aware of both the words and the body language that are part of the communication.

Sensitivity is as important in selecting the time to offer advice as it is in understanding truly what your mentee is communicating.

WHEN TO COACH

As a mentor, you need to keep your ideas to yourself until you are asked for them. This doesn't mean that you say nothing. However, specific advice regarding your mentee's job responsibilities should be held back until your mentee asks for it. Unsolicited advice on an unremitting basis only clogs the ears of a mentee. In time, your mentee will automatically disregard everything that you say.

You can trigger discussion, however, by probing with a question or two. Let's say that your mentee has an idea and has just completed describing it, crossing every *t* and dotting every *i*. As you listened, you were aware of some problems with the idea, but your mentee hasn't asked you what you think. Your feedback hasn't been requested. How, then, do you alert your mentee to the difficulties that are likely to arise? You might repeat the last sentence said by your mentee. Let's assume he has concluded his remark by saying, "That's how I plan to turn the decline in profits down."

You would say, in turn, "So that's how you plan to reverse the economic downfall." By repeating your mentee's remark, you show him that you heard his remark. But by pitching your voice a little down and saying the words slowly, you may trigger your mentee to ask the question that you were waiting to hear: "What do you think of the idea?"

You may see numerous problems with the idea but this isn't the time to enumerate each and every difficulty. Identify one or two key points that you see as critical to the idea and point them out to your mentee. If you have other concerns, you can make mention of problems three, four, and five later in your discussion. As you are discussing the idea with your mentee, you might focus on a better way to handle each of these issues. Forgo pointing to the faults and play up how approaching the idea as you suggest might improve the likelihood of the idea working.

Ideally, you want to develop a dialogue with your mentee—a one-to-one discussion that is relaxed and candid. Should you have negative feedback, many of the same rules that you use in coaching or counseling a staff member apply. Foremost, don't let your anger loose, no matter how you might feel. Because anger will work its way into the conversation even when you are doing your utmost to keep it at bay, end a meeting when you feel yourself losing your temper and reschedule the session for a time when you can approach the issue more calmly.

You also want to come across as objective and your feedback should be nonjudgmental. Sensitive mentees will likely overreact to negative feedback—even if it is strictly related to their job behavior—considering it a personal attack. If you think that I am suggesting that, instead, you find no fault with a mentee with a behavioral problem, you are wrong. Employees who are hypersensitive to any kind of negative feedback are also highly sensitive to diversionary tactics. So trying to sandwich some negative thoughts between slices of praise compounds an already awkward situation. As the mentee waits for the bad news, apprehension grows.

So how should you deliver negative feedback? You need to communicate it in an easily digestible fashion. During your first meetings with your mentee, you should make it clear that your mentee will receive feedback during your meetings. Make it clear that such feedback is meant as a developmental summary—advice to direct her toward her career aspirations. After all, no one likes operating in the dark. Even when your mentee's performance is outstanding, she should receive feedback—in this instance, positive input. Positive feedback is as important to dispense when things are going well as is negative feedback when problems are evident.

I have tried consistently in this chapter to use the term *feedback* or *constructive feedback*, not criticism or constructive criticism. Try to avoid feedback such as: "You really screwed up in leading this project." Your intention should be to offer information that your mentee can use to reinforce positive behavior and redirect negative behavior. For this reason, it must be as objective as humanly possible. The above statement, however, is subjective, critical, and certainly demoralizing.

Mentee-centered comments like this are likely to have the opposite effect. While your goal is to get your mentee to accept your feedback, focusing on the employee—repeatedly referring to the mentee as *you*—is more likely to cause your protégé to reject it. Here are some more examples of unconstructive feedback:

- "You aren't listening." This comment is one of the best ways to get your mentee to stop listening.
- "Why did you do it that way?" It doesn't matter the nature of the problem, the word *why* combined with the pronoun *you* is likely to cause the mentee to become defensive.
- "If you'll be quiet, I'll let you know what you did wrong." This is really just a slick way of asking someone to shut up.

Now that you have some idea of what not to say to your mentee, what should you say?

Your feedback needs to be honest, succinct, and lucid. You want to build the kind of rapport with your mentee that leads to greater trust and comfort, so you want to engage in small talk for a few minutes after greeting your mentee. If the feedback you are going to give—and your mentee suspects you will be giving—is negative, you shouldn't leave your mentee squirming in the seat for what seems like an eternity. If you see a problem, let your mentee know. If you suspect you know the root cause or causes, share that information as well. Discuss openly possible solutions to correcting the problem. Give your mentee time to digest the information and then listen to the reply.

Your intention in providing negative feedback is to point out where a mistake was made, but also why it was made and, most important, how the mentee logically can avoid making it in the future.

NEGATIVE AND POSITIVE LANGUAGE

The phrasing of your feedback is as important as the purpose of your feedback. Let's look, first, at some common negative phrasing.

- "You neglected to specify . . ."
- "You failed to include . . ."
- "Why did you overlook . . . ?"

- "I cannot see how you . . ."
- "I fail to see why . . ."
- "You understand, of course . . ."
- "You claim that . . ."

Note how these phrases imply carelessness, lack of intelligence, even lying.

What, then, are some positive phrases? Positive phrases suggest that your mentee has the capability to accomplish something exceptional, can turn around questionable behavior, or can rethink some viewpoint, such as:

- "One option open to you is . . ."
- "You have a different viewpoint on this matter. Let me explain my opinion."
- "I believe you could . . ."

The reason you need to be conscious of your phrasing is the consequence of your phrasing, intentional or not. Negative phrasing tells a mentee what you think he or she cannot do or subtly places blame on the mentee. It doesn't point out those actions that would be appropriate or lead to more positive consequences. Positive phrasing, on the other hand, suggests alternatives and choices available to your mentee and reflects a positive opinion of the mentee's capability.

WHEN NOT TO GIVE FEEDBACK

I've warned you to cool off before you give feedback. But there is another time when constructive feedback invariably has an adverse effect. It is when your mentee can't take any action on the constructive feedback. Consider what happened with Pat and her mentee Anna. Pat had observed Anna give a presentation. Afterward, she told her that she liked Anna's effort a lot. "There is only one problem I see. You would come across as more professional if you relied on PowerPoint rather than flipcharts and overhead projectors." Unfortunately, Anna's own manager prefers that his staff members use flipcharts and overhead slides. Anna would have liked to use PowerPoint—she knew it would have improved her presentation—but her hands were tied. This only made her frustrated. She wanted to do what Pat suggested but she had no control over the situation. Pat's suggestion also caused Anna to question how well Pat knew the other members of management, particularly her own boss. Her boss was known for his Luddite-like attitude toward use of new technology to facilitate presentations. It made Anna wonder if Pat knew what she was talking about when she offered organizational insights.

Guidelines for Giving Feedback

When you sit down with your mentee, keep the following in mind:

- Be clear about what you want to say.
- Begin with the positive. Looking at the positive will make it easier for your mentee to hear about the areas for improvement.
- Be specific. Avoid generalizations and clarify pronouns such as *it*, *that*, and the like.
- Focus on behavior rather than on the person.
- Refer to the behavior that can be changed. Don't try to change that which is not changeable.
- Be descriptive rather than evaluative.
- Own the feedback. Have the courage to use "I" statements.
- Avoid the following words: *always, never, all*, etc.
- Don't give advice. Most people won't listen. Rather, help the individual come to a better understanding of an issue and how to address it more effectively.

10 Ways You Can Anger Your Mentee

Your goal in giving feedback is to have your opinion heard and your suggestions hopefully followed. Your mentee will tend to resist feedback—even argue—when you:

1. Provide unsolicited advice. Even if your role as a mentor is to give advice, you should wait until you are asked for it.
2. Appear to want to blame rather than fix.
3. Offer reassurances that are not based on reality. Don't promise that an improvement in a given behavior will guarantee promotion, for example.

4. Offer sympathy rather than empathy.
5. Pressure a person to change by continuous repetition of the problem.
6. Seem superior by proving the mentee did something wrong.
7. Suggest that you are infallible.
8. Use words that are hot buttons—like *always* and *never*—that lead to defensive responses.
9. Hide negative feedback among positive statements.
10. Try to make the mentee feel responsible for a consequence that is beyond his or her control.

H o w T r u s t w o r t h y A r e Y o u ?

An important element to being a successful mentor is the trust others have in you. Ask yourself which statement in each pair best reflects you:

- 1a. I listen carefully to others.
- 1b. I don't always listen. Sometimes, I'm so busy that I ignore what the other person is saying.

- 2a. I share my thoughts and feelings with others.
- 2b. I hold in my personal feelings and hide my thoughts.

- 3a. I keep the promises I made. If I can't be sure of keeping a promise, I don't make a promise.
- 3b. I have been known to break promises. Sometimes, it is just easier to agree to someone's request even if I know I won't be able to deliver on it. Other times, I say yes when I can't guarantee the promise with certainty.

- 4a. I accept others' styles and personalities and make an effort to work with them.
- 4b. I tend to be hypercritical and judgmental of others.

- 5a. I am open to new ideas and information.
- 5b. I have strong views and it makes it tough for me to accept opinions and information contrary to what I believe.

(continued)

- 6a. I make an effort to build others' self-esteem and provide them with the skills, abilities, and knowledge they need to succeed.
- 6b. I don't suffer fools gladly. I will criticize and even ridicule others with ideas that I consider unworkable.

- 7a. I believe I am extremely cooperative—a real team player.
- 7b. It's a competitive world and I intend to come up first. It's the squeaky wheel that gets oiled.

- 8a. I am known to focus on my staff's strengths.
- 8b. I expect my employees to do their jobs well and won't tolerate mistakes. I let my staff know this, whatever the situation.

- 9a. I do what I say and I say what I do.
- 9b. I have been known to send mixed messages.

- 10a. I keep confidential information given me.
- 10b. I divulge confidential information.

All right, how well do you think you did? Would you rather have, as a mentor, the individual who matches the first statements in each pair (a) or the person who fits the second statements (b)? The first statements, of course, are representative of a good mentor.

ASKING GOOD QUESTIONS

I've pointed out the need to start with a setup statement and then follow up the statement, once you are both on the same page, with a number of questions. Because you want to create insight into the experience, you want to ask questions that encourage your mentee to undertake some critical thinking. Here are some key points about the nature of asking questions.

- *Monitor the time between the question being asked and the reply.* If the mentee doesn't respond in ten seconds, you need to rephrase the question. Also, keep eye contact. It will convey a sincere interest in your protégé's reply. Your intention is not to put your mentee on the spot.

- *Don't talk after you ask the question.* Give your protégé an opportunity to answer. While too much silence is dangerous, silence itself can be golden, encouraging your mentee to respond. Unless the mentee exceeds the ten seconds, assume that your protégé heard and understood the question and is simply considering his reply.
- *Think before you ask your question.* Consider the goal of your question and ask yourself if the reply will take you in the direction in which you want the conversation to go.
- *Don't lead the protégé.* That's not for mentors to do. All you will get are the answers you want to hear, not the honest answers that will move your mentee forward in achieving the development goals on which you have agreed.
- *Dig with your questions.* More in-depth inquiry may trigger a little discomfort for the mentee and yourself, but safe superficial questions will do little to provide insights into how your mentee is thinking. Actually, conflict is good if you can work through it. It will lead to interpersonal closeness and openness between you and your mentee.
- *Don't expect rapport between you and your mentee immediately.* Back off and give your protégé an opportunity to communicate thoughts. Good friends develop the kind of rapport that allows each to complete the sentence of the other. It can take many months, even years, as a mentor to someone to gain that kind of relationship. Start slowly.

T i p s   t o   H e l p   Y o u   P r o v i d e   F e e d b a c k

1. *Provide real-time feedback.* Tie your remarks to recent mentee assignments or experiences. You might say, "I have a few ideas that might help . . ." or, alternatively, "What works for me is. . . ."
2. *Keep in mind that the only feedback that's useful is about behavior that the mentee can change.* Don't succumb to the temptation to evaluate the mentee. Ask, "What impact would that behavior have on the project's success?" or say to your protégé, "Your supervisor would look at your behavior as. . . ."
3. *Be sure you understand what happened.* Listen actively. Clarify and summarize. "If I understand what you said. . . ." or, "Help me to understand what happened. . . ."

(continued)

4. *Speak with respect.* You don't want to undermine your protégé's self-esteem. Point out the positives as well as the negatives. Say, "I liked the way you. . . ." Then follow it up with, "Have you ever considered . . . ?"

5. *Be alert to your communication style's impact on your mentee.* Discuss your style with your protégé and how you can improve the interaction between you. Tell your mentee, for instance, "I find that I get defensive when . . ." or "Do you react more positively to . . . ?"

6. *Link progress to the bigger picture.* When you do this, your mentee will recognize the worth in the mentoring relationship. For instance, you might say, "When we started, you felt. . . . And then, we decided. . . . Now, we are seeing. . . ."

C a s e   S t u d y

DLR GROUP

Mentoring programs can be found in small organizations, as well as multinational firms. At DLR Group, a 600-person architectural/engineering firm with regional offices in Omaha, Seattle, Minneapolis, and Phoenix, mentoring has contributed to:

- Transition of useful knowledge
- More fluid project delivery
- Improved communication
- Guidance to staff
- Greater accountability

Uncertain whether a mentoring program would work, the organization began with a beta program, setting up mentoring relationships both across disciplines and up and down the firm's hierarchy. Those who served as mentors were expected to handle their new role during the normal course of project delivery. Mentors and protégés were selected according to each protégé's perceived need. Mentors were expected to offer hands-on assistance, not sit back like a guru and offer words of encouragement. Mentors train protégés, coach, and provide general advice.

Mentoring opportunities aren't artificially created. Rather, when they arise, they are utilized by the mentor. For instance, when a protégé travels with a mentor to a client meeting, the mentor uses the occasion to review the agenda and work with the protégé to design how the upcoming meeting will be managed. In another instance, a protégé being groomed for the role of project manager is able to query his project architect mentor on the project's status. Reverse mentoring is also utilized. In one instance, a junior expert in CAD mentored a senior project manager who wanted but lacked CAD skills.

The beta test by the firm focused on key aspects of project management, from subjects like speaking and effective listening to team building and client management. In terms of administrative skills, mentoring covered budgeting, negotiations, risk management, meeting management, and the like.

The pilot program proved so successful that the program was expanded to cover three other disciplines covered in the firm's Phoenix office—education, criminal justice, and private sector commercial construction.

6

THE E-DIMENSION

Office technology has created challenges for businesses but it has also created opportunities. Certainly, that's the case with mentoring. Mentors need not wait to exchange information in person. Rather, they can communicate via e-mail or voicemail, intranet or Internet. Software exists that will set up discussion boards through which mentors and protégés can have ongoing dialogues.

And let's not forget cell phones for emergency calls for advice.

Because electronic communication can be as effective as face-to-face communication, a manager quickly can answer a question or offer advice on a work problem rather than wait for the next scheduled meeting. Most important, the technology allows mentoring relationships to exist where those involved work in different locations—not only in different offices but even in different countries.

For instance, in Hewlett-Packard's highest level leadership development programs, high-potential/high-performing mentees are paired with people who can most help them excel. Those senior managers and individual achievers are often on the other side of the globe. Microsoft does the same in its innovative companywide career mentoring initiative. The Association of Research Librarians and the Center for Health Leadership link mentor-mentee partnerships across states and time zones. (For more about global mentoring, see the sidebar at the end of this chapter.)

Even if mentors and mentees work in the same location, both may spend most of their time traveling. Consequently, they must use distance mentoring.

Technology also allows executives and managers to be mentors to individuals outside their company—from disadvantaged youngsters who need positive role models to talented students studying to enter the same field. In Florida, as a case in point, managers—from CEOs to employees—volunteer to mentor youngsters for an hour a week. Under the direction of Governor Bush, the program has drawn over 250 companies from different industries to participate in a program as dependent on e-mail mentoring as face-to-face communications.

In Austin, Texas, of 3,000 mentors for high school students, 300 are e-mentors. There are another 1,000 tech workers on a waiting list for next year's mentoring program. The employees come from a diverse group of businesses, including Austin Energy, IBM, and the University of Texas. Through regular e-mails, the technology-minded grownups keep in touch with grade school students and try to reinforce the value of education.

Direct Contact Online Volunteers (http://www.serviceleader.org) is one of many Web sites that seeks out volunteer mentors, tutors, advisors, and others to work with clients (including students) for a variety of purposes, from "visiting" someone who is homebound to providing online mentoring and instruction, such as helping a student with a homework question or a young adult learn a skill or find a job. Volunteers through this site also help people learn English as a second language, manage a support line, provide advance "welcomes" to people about to enter a hospital or to begin summer camp, and offer post-education training as part of a blended learning experience.

Distance mentoring is a term that has been used as a synonym for e-mentoring. *Virtual mentoring* is another term. In many ways, distance or virtual mentoring is very similar to traditional mentoring except that the mentor may be in one city and the mentee in another. One protégé told me, "My mentor lives in a different city, but we've been able to make our relationship work. We both decided this would be a key priority. The other day, my mentor sent me an e-mail with a great article on business management as an attachment. I couldn't believe that she took the time to do that. It made me feel as if my mentor really wanted me to advance in my career."

The relationship has been successful because the mentor has wanted to make it so. Research has also shown benefits of virtual mentoring over traditional mentoring. A virtual mentoring program provides for greater flexibility in regard to time because when two people are separated by multiple time zones, the number of hours they may be available to each other decreases. Also, it allows individuals from very different parts of the country to partner, which can make the experience broadening for both.

At the same time, there are drawbacks to virtual mentoring. The experience can lack the spontaneity of interpersonal communication that usually develops in face-to-face mentoring. A mentee told me that when she would ask for assistance locating some Web resources her mentor might take several days to comply. When a mentor found something that he thought was of value, he would e-mail it to the mentee. A few more days or in some instances weeks went by before he would hear back from the protégé. In the interim, the mentor admitted that he had lost some of his enthusiasm for the topic. Had he been able to meet face-to-face, the response would have been immediate and the pair would have been able to generate more interest in the subject, maybe even identifying further opportunities for the mentee to grow professionally.

This shouldn't discourage prospective mentors from considering this mode of mentorship. Those who have engaged in virtual mentoring programs report that their experience was a fun challenge. They felt they had grown themselves because the process put a little greater demand on their communication skills—in particular, their ability to get their ideas across through e-mail.

UNDERSTANDING THE PROCESS

There are four key steps in most mentoring relationships, and they are as applicable in distance mentoring as in traditional mentor relationships.

1. Building the relationship
2. Setting clear expectations
3. Monitoring results
4. Providing feedback

Let's look at each step from the perspective of distance mentoring.

Building the Relationship

While sending e-mail may be quick and easy, it shouldn't be the only form of communication. Ideally, it shouldn't be the first form of communication. If possible, both the mentor and protégé should meet in person to share their objectives from the relationship. Look for business reasons to be in the same city, and then schedule a mentoring meeting there. If possible, also schedule a social engagement with each other once in a while. Even if you just meet at a coffee shop briefly, it can go a long way toward bonding your relationship.

If that is impossible, then this bonding process must be handled via electronic communication, either by phone or e-mail. As a consequence, the relationship may grow at a slower pace than a traditional, face-to-face relationship. It will take more effort and time for both parties to feel comfortable with the other and for trust to grow between them, but experience has shown that such relationships can work as well as traditional mentoring relationships over the long term. If you can't meet, however, consider sharing a picture of yourself. Most people are curious about what the person on the other end of the phone or computer looks like, and sharing a picture can help assuage this curiosity.

Setting Clear Expectations

Ask your protégé if he or she has specific concerns or career goals. Share as well how you hope to assist the individual. In addition, be clear about your commitment to your protégé. Some protégés assume that you will be more accessible because you both are communicating via e-mail, but that may actually not be the case.

Planning is crucial to the success of any mentoring relationship but especially one conducted long distance. If communication is via phone, then we are talking not only about the importance of planning to the mentoring relationship but also the importance of planning each and every conversation to ensure that both mentor and protégé go away from the phone conversation feeling that something was accomplished.

In the beginning of the relationship, you and your mentee should decide the frequency with which you will communicate. Just as facilitated mentoring programs have contracts that define levels of commitment, including when, how, and what will be communicated by the parties, you may want to do the same in your virtual mentoring relationship. With a schedule in place for communications, you will avoid falling into the "out of sight, out of mind" trap that can harm long-distance relationships.

When necessary, update the document to keep you on track and your commitment fresh.

Don't cancel a meeting except for an emergency. If you must cancel, reschedule immediately. Give responsibility for managing the meetings to the mentee. This includes sending a proposed agenda in advance, making sure to start and end on time, and summarizing the discussion and agreements before ending the session.

Monitoring Results

Some mentors and protégés communicate exclusively via e-mail, while others limit e-mail communications to the posing of questions to the mentor for which they do not need an immediate response, requests for meetings with the other party, and summaries of conclusions drawn from the last communication. All other communications are handled via phone.

Those who run phone meetings, kick off these phone sessions with a review of the protégé's last assignment or outcome of the planned activity discussed during the last phone call. What did the protégé accomplish? Is there something new that the protégé tried that was successful? What challenges did the protégé overcome and what challenges does he or she still feel need to be met? What did the mentee learn about how to handle a new responsibility and about himself or herself?

The mentor and protégé should also review any unexpected situations that arose since the last phone call. What were they? What impact have they had on the opportunities or challenges facing the protégé in the near future? How can the mentor help?

Finally, the two should discuss those activities the protégé will be doing until the next phone call. The protégé should be prepared to identify the next learning opportunity, and together the mentoring partners should decide on an appropriate assignment as a learning experience. Before the two hang up, they should agree on a date when the two will talk again at which time the protégé will offer an update on the assignment.

There's nothing wrong with putting a little spontaneity into the relationship either. As mentor, call your protégé to check in, say hello, or ask how things are going. Likewise, encourage your protégé to call you to share good news. Even if the phone is your predominant method of communicating, e-mail is also a great way to keep in touch. If you and your protégé have discussed a new task the protégé must face and you've come across an article on the Internet that can help, send the URL.

Providing Feedback

Because distance management doesn't give a mentor the same interaction with a protégé as face-to-face communications, the mentor has to rely on the remote control that comes from respect for the mentor. The mentor can begin to foster that trust by showing trust in the protégé. That means that you question your protégé about the results of an assignment only when there is real reason to do so.

Before you commit to distance mentoring, determine what communication technology would be available to you. There are a number of options—e-mail, instant messaging, the telephone, video conferencing, and Web conferencing, just to name a few. Ask yourself with which you would be most comfortable working.

In providing feedback via phone, you should listen for nonverbal signals. Sometimes you can tell how your protégé feels about what you are saying not by what she is saying but how she is saying it. Keep your ear tuned for a rising or lowering of her voice, a change in tone, a quickening or slowing of speaking pace, sighs, pauses, and, worst of all, ominous silence.

In face-to-face communications, as we discussed in Chapter 5, "Straight Talk," response to your words will be evident by body language. In phone communications, you will need to tell your protégé what you are "hearing" or "sensing." Clarify feelings by asking your protégé how she feels about your remark.

Push for specifics—don't settle for generalities. Ask that your protégé express thoughts and opinions clearly and with focus. After all, you have to understand where your protégé is coming from to make the mentoring relationship worthwhile for you both.

Certainly, don't hang up before you have both summarized in your own words the specifics to which you have agreed, testing the accuracy of your perceptions.

When you are communicating via e-mail, just as on the phone, you should be focused on the communications under way. Don't let coworkers distract you from the flow of communications. If your company has the technology, you may want to use Web cameras and online conference options for electronic face-to-face meetings to handle coaching sessions. Certainly, in providing constructive feedback, think first before you press the "Send" button.

This is worthy of further discussion.

Long-Distance Communication

First and foremost, don't e-mail a response to a mentee's message if you are uncertain about the message the mentee sent you. There are times when it is better to phone instead of to write an e-mail, and one crucial time is when you want to hear the person's voice tone so you can "read between the lines" about the message sent. If your mentee is upset about your earlier message or some event in life, a personal phone call is preferable to an e-mail message inquiring about what happened.

You may be tempted to respond immediately to a message, either via e-mail or on an instant messaging system. Don't. Avoid knee-jerk responses.

Electronic communication is quick—that's why we use it. But its greatest benefit can also be its greatest drawback. When you sit down at the keyboard to respond to your e-mail, your mind-set is typically to get through everything—to empty your mailbox and free yourself for other tasks.

That mind-set can generate knee-jerk responses. So be mindful of speed when you are answering e-mail from your mentee—a terse, quickly worded response to a critical question can destroy the considerable time you have taken to build a positive relationship with your distance mentee.

You want your communications to resemble a face-to-face conversation, but be cautious that you don't come across as too informal, even careless and indifferent.

Again, the problem rests with the technology. It enables us to be informal—to use a conversational tone, a breezy style, colloquial words and phrases, sentence fragments, abbreviations, and even acronyms. All of these are conventions you might use in face-to-face conversations with someone, and they are appropriate in some kinds of e-mail.

However, being informal can be seen as indifference by a mentee who has sent a plea for help to you. Likewise, unclear and incomplete thoughts, ambiguous references, irrelevant details, disorganized ideas, and grammatical errors all say that you don't care about the mentee enough to treat the query with some respect. Grammatical mistakes or misspellings may seem petty compared to the message itself, but deciphering a confusing and poorly written message can only irritate someone already emotionally in distress.

A rule to keep in mind: If your e-mail is worth composing and sending, it's worth writing well enough to be understood.

Think before you write your response to a mentee's e-mail message, assuming that you believe that it is an appropriate or convenient way to address the individual's question. We'll discuss the message itself, but let me add one final warning associated with the Send button.

People occasionally hit Send prematurely or accidentally, sending an unedited or half-written e-mail. If this is a common error of yours, let me suggest that you hold off entering the recipient's e-mail address until you have completed the message. Read it through once or twice to be sure that it is sensitive to the mentee's need and also reflects well on your reputation before you add the address and then hit the Send button.

If you receive a message and decide to reply to it, be alert that most systems automatically insert the sender's e-mail address. If this is the case, you may need to remove the address manually until you are ready to send your reply. This way, if you unintentionally press Send, your e-mail will still remain safely on your screen and not in the recipient's mailbox.

DON'T YELL

Let's look at the appearance of the message as well as the technology. Avoid using all uppercase letters. Writers that use all uppercase or lowercase think it's faster to keyboard without hitting the Shift key, and they are right—it is faster for them as the sender. But it isn't faster for the reader. Further, Web savvy readers view messages in uppercase letters as a form of yelling which is not the kind of impression you want the mentee to get from your message.

While adding a double space between paragraphs if your reply is a lengthy one aids an e-mail's readability, don't double-space your entire message. Readers need to grasp sentences, paragraphs, and lists as single units and double-spacing makes that difficult.

What about the use of emoticons or "smileys"? For trivial e-mail, emoticons may be appropriate. But when communicating about serious topics—serious to the mentee, if not to you—don't use them. They'll detract from your professionalism and distract the reader.

If you need to send a sensitive message, and you think a smiley will help overcome some unpleasant feedback or information, be sure that the smiley will do the trick. A smiley won't disguise an offensive remark as a joke. The recipient may not know the particular smiley, either. After almost a decade of e-mail, emoticons are proliferating, and their meanings are by no means universal.

You also should keep humor out of your e-mail replies to mentees. You may want to soften a remark, or try to add that twinkle in the eye or shrug of the shoulders that acts as a clue in face-to-face communications, but such subtle humor isn't easy to convey through e-mail. If you aren't sure that your attempt at humor will work, or you feel the need to add one of those sideways smiley faces to signal to the reader that you are joking, it is better to not try your wit at all.

TONE, RHYTHM, PERSUASION

How can you communicate effectively via e-mail? The key is to write in a friendly tone. This means that you should make an effort to duplicate a conversational style in your e-mail without erring on the side of being too informal and conversational. Use words and phrases that come naturally. Avoid the tendency to overwrite.

Contractions will help to make your message seem friendly. A contraction lets you achieve a warmer, down-to-earth tone in a sentence. Deciding when to use a contraction is a matter of taste and style, but here are some rules that may help.

- Use a contraction if you'd use it when speaking the sentence aloud.
- Replace a few of the contractions with the full words if you find your writing contains too many of them.
- Be aware of hidden wordiness in contractions; for instance, "*I've got* a book that might help you" should be "*I have* a book that might help you."
- Avoid using clumsy or seldom-used contractions such as: The head of the *firm'll* get you for that costly error.
- Use full words or phrases if you want a more formal tone or if you want to add special emphasis to a phrase.

You want to come across as concerned about your mentee, but that shouldn't prompt you to insert what are sometimes called *weasel words* into your communications. Weasel words enable the writer to obscure information—even avoid responsibility. For instance, an unsure mentor might write, "For all intents and purposes, I would think you have completed the goal we set." On the other hand, if the mentor truly believed that the mentee had completed the agreed-on goal satisfactorily, he or she would have written, "I believe that you completed the goal we set." See the sidebar to find a number of other hedging words.

Some other negative phrases or words to avoid include: fail, wrong, unless, never, not, none, according to, claim, neglected to, and lack of.

The ideal is to create rhythm in your e-mail. If there is negative news, begin with it, followed by any positive information. Use a mixture of short, medium, and long sentences. If you have a sentence that seems too long, consider breaking it into two smaller sentences. To test whether a sentence is too long, read it aloud. If you run out of breath, the sentence is definitely too long.

Most important, consider the reader's reaction to your message. If you are sending an e-mail message that may cause the reader to lose face, then you need to make a conscious effort to be as tactful and objective as possible. Find a way to let your reader save dignity. If you can't, you'll need to include supporting evidence. If you are critiquing the mentee, you might want to share one of your similar experiences. It should help to make the negative feedback a little easier to swallow.

If the individual takes issue with your response, suggest a phone call to discuss the matter further. If you will be getting together soon and you don't believe delaying further discussion will impede the mentee's developmental progress, suggest you discuss it then.

If you've done all you can to deliver the message with care and consideration for the recipient, that's all you can really do. Rarely do writers find unbiased readers. That is, most readers have a stake in the subject matter of your writing—none more so than a mentee reading feedback from a mentor. Determining the strength of your reader's biases may actually give you insight into the mentoring effort ahead for you.

Are You Guilty of Hedging?

Don't lengthen your e-mail by adding these weasel words or namby-pamby modifiers. If your goal is to make your point clearly, why clutter your message with words like *very* and *seemingly*? If you are using any of the words or phrases from the list below, determine if they add anything to the comprehension of an e-mail or if they simply convey an uncomfortable sense that you are not saying something that should be said.

rather	pretty
seemingly	little
somewhat	it would seem
kind of	in some respects
mostly	for the most part
very	for all intents and purposes.

Issues and Challenges in E-Mentoring

One way to assess your long-distance relationship with your mentee is to begin by identifying some of the challenges that are associated with mentoring over a long distance (e.g., time commitment, sensitivity to day-to-day needs of mentor and mentee, effectiveness of communication). These can be listed in the "Issues" column in the table below. Next, in the column under "Mentor," evaluate how well you believe you have addressed the issue either from your own perspective or as a half of a pair. Then ask your mentee to do the same in the column marked "Mentee." Ideally, meet to discuss the conclusions. If that's impossible, set aside quiet time for an in-depth telephone conversation to assess each individual's viewpoint.

Issue	Mentor	Mentee

A c t i o n   P l a n   f o r   E - M e n t o r i n g

What to Do	How to Do It
Invest time and effort in setting the climate for learning.	Discuss with your mentee how he or she believes you can maximize time together. Determine learning needs and agree on goals.
Be sensitive to the day-to-day needs of your mentee.	Ask questions in order to fully understand your mentee's workload, and ensure that your protégé will have sufficient time to complete each development assignment you provide.
Identify venues for communication.	Explore all available options: e-mail, telephone, and emerging technology. Look for opportunities to connect face to face.
Set a regular contact schedule.	Agree on a mutually convenient schedule and make sure it works not only for you but also your mentee. If you need to change a meeting time, alert your mentee sufficiently in advance. Communicate to your mentee your desire to do the same.
Assess the effectiveness of communication.	Ask questions to ensure that you are both on the same page. You want to be sure that the advice and counsel you offer as a mentor are paying off for the mentee.

The Global Dimension

Electronic communication has facilitated mentoring across borders. In particular, mentoring programs are being used to help expatriates develop the cultural astuteness they need to work effectively abroad. Those on overseas assignments welcome being in contact with someone from headquarters who can keep them informed of developments that might influence their careers. It's even better if those abroad are familiar with the cultures of their new locales or some of the problems they might encounter in their new assignments.

When a mentor's purpose is to prepare the protégé with some appreciation of the culture in which the mentee will work, whether the assignment is short or long term, the mentor needs to alert the protégé to nine factors that, acting one upon another, create the culture of a country or region.

1. Religion
2. Education
3. Economics
4. Politics
5. Family
6. Language
7. Class Structure
8. History
9. Geography

Let's assume that you find yourself in the position of being asked to mentor someone from another culture who will soon be relocating to the U.S. or, alternatively, you are being asked to mentor someone from another country who will be relocating to a third country, one in which you worked for several years. In the first instance, you are being asked to prepare your new colleague for the job in the U.S. In the second case, you are expected to help your peer get through those awkward first months in the new location—to prepare for the move. Your communications with these individuals will primarily be via e-mail.

Be assured that you'll make unintentional mistakes. As you get to know your mentee, you may begin to forget that you don't value the same rules of protocol, time and punctuality, authority figures, decision-making processes, or humor, and, consequently, you may send a message that is unintentionally offensive. If it happens, it happens. Apologize immediately, work to rebuild any broken bridge with the individual, and continue your effort toward making your mentee very much a part of the team.

Keep in mind too that people from different cultures organize information differently. For instance, people from East Asian cultures tend to organize material based on relationships of elements rather than the linear progression typical of Western thinking. There are also differences in the West. Canadians, for instance, like to have recommendations at the beginning of a communication; the remainder of the message supports the recommendation. The emphasis is on the practical use of information. Germans, on the other hand, prefer information to be organized chronologically. They give the background first, then the recommendation. The French seem to revel in providing rationale for their recommendations—which means a lengthy and flowery presentation of their argument.

In the United States, many words and idioms stem from the military. Businesses have strategies, they go on the offensive, they plan the attack, they dig in, they have price wars, they destroy the enemy (corporate competitors), they rally the troops, they are on the defensive or the offensive, they have intelligence-gathering systems, and so forth. Most Americans use this terminology without an awareness of its roots. To people from more reserved and peaceful cultures, e-mail filled with such idioms will seem combative and aggressive. Tone down your e-mail and choose more cooperative phrases when communicating to your protégé.

Likewise, sports analogies, in particular those from baseball and football, have provided us with countless metaphors. Men and women in American business, even non-sports fans, incorporate it into their business vocabulary. They assume that everyone understands what is meant when they use sentences such as:

- The company hit a home run.
- We got to first base.
- Management sent him down to the minors.
- My colleague struck out.
- She has a good batting average.
- We want a level playing field.
- All the bases are covered.
- We don't like Monday-morning quarterbacking.
- We celebrated a touchdown.

If there is a single message about global mentoring, it is this: Be culturally sensitive. While e-mail lends itself to an informal and personal writing style, that style may turn off someone who comes from a more formal cultural background. Consequently, the more you know about your protégé's native culture, the easier it will be to communicate.

H ow D o Y ou F are in
C ross - Cultural C ommunication ?

Below we have identified through ten questions several skills critical to cross-cultural communication. In the second column, indicate examples of what you have done that enables you to answer yes to each question. In the third column, evaluate your level of success. A check mark suggests that you are doing well in that area. If you feel more effort is needed in certain areas, fill out in the section labeled Action Plan describing how you intend to improve in each area.

Skill Question	What Have You Done?	How Am I Doing?
1. Have I researched my mentee's culture?		
2. Have I used reflective listening to clarify and confirm what I have heard?		
3. Have I checked that my protégé understands my remarks?		
4. Am I reading nonverbal messages (such as pauses and silences)?		
5. Am I suspending judgment until I have clarified communication?		
6. Overall, am I providing and receiving feedback?		
7. Am I sensitive to feelings—mine and those of my protégé?		
8. Have I modified my communication style to accommodate cultural differences?		
9. Have I been alert to my protégé's perceptions of authority and protocol?		
10. Am I developing a global perspective?		

Action Plans:

Question # _____

Question # _____

Question # _____

C a s e S t u d y

INTEL'S HR MENTORING PROGRAM

Intel is an organization that has decided to expand its initial mentoring program. Its earlier program used a manual system to match mentees and mentors using skills assessments each participant completed.

Today's Managing Through People program has a database attached to its intranet with filters in the system that keep mentees from being matched with mentors in their chain of command. Also, lower-grade-level mentees are matched with higher-grade-level mentors.

The business reasons for implementing its newest mentoring program for HR personnel are:

- Career advancement
- New manager or leader development
- Skills transfer

Before launching this program, the HR planning team looked at the activities of other Intel mentoring programs, prepared for two months, and delivered its mentoring proposal to the corporate HR staff in Santa Clara, California. The HR VP and staff signed off immediately. The HR team held training sessions and posted information on Intel's HR intranet to make sure participants understood the objectives and processes for the mentoring program. Pilot group members were surveyed before and after they finished the six-month pilot test. Based on the group's reports of good outcomes, the program was expanded so it could accommodate the mentoring needs of all 2,000 HR employees at Intel offices across the globe.

More than 200 HR employees have participated to date in the program. At least 50 percent of the mentoring pairs have been between mentors and mentees at different geographic sites, but even the long-distance mentoring relationships have yielded good results. Online surveys, conducted once or twice a year, show high satisfaction rates—with 70 percent to 90 percent of mentees meeting their goals. Mentees report improving skills such as their decision-making ability and developing interpersonal, team building, PC, and Web-related skills.

Those responsible for the program attribute its success to upper management support, an easy-to-use system with good documentation, and adequate numbers of mentors available. The company also offers online training so participants can learn more about mentoring processes.

7

MENTORING THROUGH DIFFICULT SITUATIONS

Sometimes, constructive feedback isn't enough. Advice offered may be rejected. The problem may be in the coaching effort, the personality of either partner, or the nature of the relationship. The more unique the relationship, the more likely a problem may develop between the participants. Whether you decide to end, renew, or revive the mentoring relationship as a consequence, it must be done consciously, intentionally, and openly.

POSITIONAL POWER VERSUS MENTORING POWER

It's important to remember when coaching a mentee that your relationship is very different from that of a supervisor. You possess positional power in your relationships with your employees, whereas in a mentee you have only a willingness to listen and follow your advice based on your experience and the trust between you. The mentee may not always go along with your advice. Sometimes, the mentee may simply disagree with what you are suggesting. If you are criticizing some specific behavior, the mentee may even consider that you are wrong and deny the problem.

Clearly, the problem with giving criticism—even what we call "constructive feedback"—is that some people just don't take kindly to it. Criticism is evaluative and judgmental, no matter how much you might try to sugarcoat it with the advice given in Chapter 5.

Most people feel threatened by criticism. For some, it can even prolong the problem. What should you do? Avoiding giving the criticism would mean accepting the defeating behavior, so that is not the right response. When a mentee's behavior isn't up to snuff, you need to address it. Your goal is to bring your mentee around to change rather than continually criticize what the mentee is doing. Giving the same criticism over and over when a mentee makes a mistake repeatedly will accomplish nothing.

In this instance, clearly, the message isn't getting through. The most effective way to handle the situation is to look at what happened and to try to analyze the source of the problem. More encouragement won't work. More complaining may only make the problem worse. While you might point to the consequences of continued repetition of the wrong behavior, if the mentee doesn't see the behavior as wrong, the feedback won't carry much weight.

If you find yourself in this situation, you need to switch from a coaching to a counseling mode. This means that you and your mentee need to do two things:

1. Agree that there is a need for a change.
2. Work together to determine specific actions that will correct the mistake or behavior problem.

If you were your mentee's supervisor, you would be able to use the threat of termination if there is no change in behavior. But as the individual's mentor, you have to rely more on the trust between you, the respect the mentee has for your past experiences, and your ability to influence the mentee's thinking.

The last point is critical. Influencing isn't about manipulation or the misuse of power. When you establish and maintain a good relationship with your mentee, he or she will be more receptive to your ideas and willing to consider your suggestions—you are using influencing skills. When you present your ideas logically and persuasively—that is, by spelling out clearly and honestly how your mentee is going to personally benefit from doing as you suggest—you are also using influencing skills.

Begin by clarifying your key objective, to make it clear, in your own mind, exactly what you want to achieve. The second step is to actually plan your campaign. In this instance, it is how you will discuss the situation with your mentee in a manner that is more likely to gain agreement. For instance, when you next meet with your mentee, you need to actively listen to what she has to say and ask open-ended questions (e.g., How?, Why?, What?, When?, and Where?) to discover any concerns that may be behind her refusal to accept your suggestions.

You also have to be prepared to thoroughly answer questions asked of you. Finally, and most important, you need to spell out the benefits to your mentee if she shifts gears and behaves as you suggest. Use open and friendly body language—maintain eye contact, keep arms in a relaxed position—to communicate your good intentions nonverbally.

Your mentee may be refusing to accept your opinion because she feels threatened, is frightened of making a mistake, or believes you are overselling your concern about the impact that continuation of such behavior will have on her career plans. Of course, it could also be that your mentee doesn't really understand what you mean.

How do you begin?

Let me describe what Michael did to convince Claire to accept that her continued domination of a new product development team in the organization was not the way to gain senior management's attention. Even if the organization was successful with the idea that she was pushing down the throats of her teammates, no one would consider her a team player, a value highly prized at their organization.

When Claire joined Michael for lunch, he began the meeting by stating, "Claire, there's something that's concerning me and I need to talk to you about it." Having heard Michael raise before the issue of her behavior with the new product development team, Claire told him, "Let's not go over that again, Mike. Management respects strong leaders."

"Yes, management respects strong leaders but," he continued, "it is looking for leaders who listen to their followers and gain their support, not those who badger and harass those with whom they work." Michael then went on to describe the management styles of several recently promoted managers. Each had gained senior management's attention by their leadership skills, yes, but these skills included a willingness to listen to their staff members, an openness to others' ideas, and creation of a strong team. "Would you agree, Claire, that these are qualities that separate these managers from others?" Michael asked his mentee.

"Yes," Claire agreed, "but that's just not my style. Michael," she continued, "I'm not sure I could handle that style effectively." Michael knew that having Claire admit her fears was a critical turning point in the discussion with his mentee. "I'll help you," he offered.

Michael and Claire then sat down and worked out an action plan that would help build the leadership skills that their organization expected of its middle managers. The development plan that they completed included specific steps that Claire should take to open discussion in the product development team so that the final recommendation of the group was a product of everyone's ideas. Because Michael had sat through several sessions in the past as a guest of the team, he promised to sit through several more sessions to observe Claire's behavior (to shadow her) and offer constructive feedback after the fact.

Claire lacked self-confidence about her ability to change her style, so Michael suggested she try to revisualize her behavior. "Think about how you would act and what you would say," he advised Claire. Michael knew that the picture she would create in her mind would help forge a real-life change in her behavior.

This didn't mean that the problem was solved. It took several more meetings for a change in Claire's behavior to become apparent. But she had gone from fighting Michael about the matter to accepting his viewpoint and asking for feedback about her behavior. He made an effort to present his thoughts clearly and logically. He invited questions and answered them patiently and thoroughly. He knew Claire had a big adjustment to make in her management/leadership style so he gave her more meeting time during this period.

Michael's influencing strategy worked because he accepted that it was a four-step process:

1. *Hear the message.* You have to overcome objections that can range from agendas different from yours to a belief that your idea is not in the mentee's best interest to an unspoken fear that giving up one behavioral style for another could lose the mentee control of a situation critical to his advancement.

2. *Understand the message.* As a mentor, you need to be sure that you are clear to your mentee about what change you expect in his behavior—and why.

3. *Get agreement.* This is your goal. Just as in counseling an employee, you can't expect a change in behavior until the mentee acknowledges that a continuation of the misbehavior can have a negative impact. It's your responsibility to communicate the cost to your mentee in a manner that isn't threatening but convinces him or her to change behavior.

4. *Take action.* You review the development goals set earlier in the relationship and adapt the list accordingly. Thereafter, you make sure you keep track of your mentee's progress. Be patient—your mentee may not change overnight. What you want to see is effort in the new direction you have both set.

A trick that many communication specialists suggest is an "I message confrontation." What's this? Let's assume that your mentee has told you that he plans to tell off a supervisor in another department. Yes, he wants to let Frank have it. What should you say? An "I message" generally contains three parts:

1. A neutral description of what you perceive the mentee intends to do.
2. A statement of the possible negative effects on the mentee or other people.
3. The feelings or emotions you are having about the mentee's plan.

Note that nowhere do you tell the mentee how to behave. The mentee still makes the final decision. However, your mentee knows the following from your "I statements":

1. "I believe you are so angry at Frank that you will march into his office and lose your temper as you tell him off."
2. "I believe others will observe your behavior and consider you unprofessional for losing your temper, no matter how justified."
3. "As your mentor, I am concerned about how such an act will impact your reputation as someone who is cool, calm, and capable of addressing numerous problematic situations."

Can you see how these three statements might discourage a mentee from pursuing his original intent?

THE RELATIONSHIP

Sometimes, the problem may be deeper than a disagreement in viewpoint between you and your mentee. For instance, the mentee may be unhappy about your relationship yet she may be unable to discuss the problem between you. For instance, the mentee may believe that you haven't devoted the time, energy, or effort to your relationship. Like many protégés, she may find it hard to talk about it. After all, the mentee will reason that you have volunteered to help her. The mentee doesn't want to seem ungrateful for your efforts. But, likely, the mentee's feelings will come out in another, subtler fashion, like irritation about your feedback, or even anger. Further, the anger will come out no matter the nature of the behavioral or developmental issue you are discussing, becoming a pattern.

At that point, you need to get to the nature of the real problem. How do you do this? As I often have to tell people, the easiest way to learn something is to ask: "What is the problem?" "How can I help you?" If you remain quiet, the silence is likely to prompt your mentee to speak up.

Likely, the mentee will begin by telling you all that she appreciates. For instance, she might say, "I like that when I bring up a concern I have, you really take me and the issue seriously and offer ideas." Or she might say, "I know how busy you are and yet you find time for me. I wish I could tell you how much I appreciate your support." Your goal is to get your mentee beyond that. Ask her, "What could I do more?" or "What could I do differently."

You may be surprised at the response. Your mentee may ask for more time with you, tell you that you lecture too much, or point out that it would be more helpful to her if you didn't describe so thoroughly your solutions and ideas and, instead, wait to hear her ideas and then critique them.

If this is the nature of the problem between you and your mentee, then it may be time to set new operating guidelines for the relationship. Revisit the goals of the partnership to see how you can work more effectively together. If the mentee is too demanding of your time or wants your time but not your viewpoints, then you may want to reassess the relationship, even consider ending it. Often, you and your mentee will find that periodic feedback from her about the relationship is as productive to its health as is your coaching, role modeling, brokering, and advocacy.

FAILURE

What if your mentee fails despite your advice? Let's consider what might have happened if Claire changed her leadership style yet was passed over for the promotion she thought she had earned. Under such circumstances, Michael would have to be supportive, pointing to the other reasons why she might not have been considered and also how she can overcome those shortcomings to be ready for the next promotion opportunity. Certainly, he should not accept blame due to his recommendation that she change her leadership style. He may have to admit a reality of mentoring to his protégé: Sometimes protégés don't get what they want.

Actually, a wise mentor expects a protégé to be less than perfect, especially one in the formative years. The trust between mentor and mentee should be such, however, that the mentee has no fear of being rejected by the mentor as a consequence. Indeed, it is helpful early in the relationship for the mentor and mentee to discuss failure—including the freedom to fail and not be rejected—in general terms before the inevitable occurs.

Incidentally, mentors also fail on occasion. Likewise, a mentor should have no fear of being rejected by the protégé as a consequence. What kind of failure? How about the possibility of a very talented, credible, experienced executive being passed over for promotion, even demoted? They are realities in today's workplace but are often not a reflection on the talents, abilities, or competencies of the executive.

If you believe your relationship with your protégé is such that she might leave you if your career is temporarily derailed, then you might want to think about looking for another protégé, one who sees her part in the partnership.

PERSONALITY CONFLICTS

Each and every one of us has at least one individual with whom we always seem to be at odds. How about you? It can be extremely awkward if that person turns out to be your mentee, yet it can happen. Over time, you discover that the individual with whom you are paired grates on your nerves personally. Earlier, I told you that chemistry between you and your mentee is definitely an asset but you can have an effective mentoring relationship without it. You don't even have to like your mentee.

Linda, a mentee, was paired with Pete at her company. She told me, "We had totally different styles. I thought he was arrogant and he thought I was uncooperative." They had a tough first year trying to make the mentoring relationship work. It took that long for both to see the worth in the other. Linda told me, "One day, I don't know why, but I realized how much I could learn from him." The same was true for Pete. "Linda has lots of technical knowledge, but she also has this ability of networking and building positive relationships with others," he said. Pete decided to take Linda with him to meet with potential and new clients. He found opportunities for her to meet important people, and he took her to contract negotiations and gave her a critical role in negotiations. "I learned a lot by watching Pete," Linda said. "We still talk on a regular basis today although I now work for another firm. We ended up not only liking each other but becoming friends."

Linda and Pete were fortunate. They had personality problems but they were able to get past them. Should you find personality conflicts between you and your mentee, you may want to give the relationship a try before walking away. It will also help you to better understand what is behind personality conflicts.

If you think of people in terms of personality style, they actually fall into four categories: task-oriented, socializer, visionary, and conceptualizer.

Task-oriented. This individual has a need for background information and other data before taking action on something. He is knowledgeable about his work, and enjoys the reputation as an expert in his field, capable of preventing or solving problems in his area of expertise. He relies on to-do lists to ensure his efficiency, and he is very focused on his work. He likes a work challenge and is proud of his loyalty to the job—sometimes, he sacrifices his own self-interest and the needs of his family in the name of loyalty to his work.

Socializer. This individual is warm, friendly, helpful, and caring about colleagues. Affiliation-oriented, she wants to be part of the group, and she resents anyone or anything that makes her feel like she's an outsider. If she feels that her mentor is questioning her support of the group, it upsets her. It is important that she meet daily over lunch with her pals to talk about the work she is doing and the events in her department and in her friends' work areas, making it tough for her to hold weekly meetings with her mentor to discuss her progress on development goals.

Visionary. This is someone who is a leader or a potential leader, continually pushing the envelope either with respect to the work or to his performance. He's interested in learning and doing more and ultimately moving up in the organization. For him, a challenge would be to be put in charge of a team and be given the opportunity to accomplish something important (in his opinion) to the organization. He likes it when he is complimented for his professional image and his foresight and creativity. He has lots of friends in the organization, but his major motivation is the desire for the power to make a difference.

On the negative side, he has grand schemes but gives little thought to implementation of these ideas. He makes assumptions without verifying them, and he has become too dependent on his mentor to come up with ways to get his ideas implemented. He has little interest in getting the training he needs to gain the skills and knowledge he will require to advance professionally. He feels his affiliations and political savvy are all he needs.

The conceptualizer. This individual tends to see the big picture, and she often needs others to fill in the details. Conceptualizers can take many forms, from a contradictor who expects to be consulted for every decision in implementing the grand plan (regardless of the efficiency of doing so), to an autocrat, unwilling to risk errors and insistent that everything be done as she demands, to a nervous wretch who hovers over those to whom it was delegated to implement the abstract concept or idea. A conceptualizer—specifically, a contradictor—is tough to mentor. The mentor will spend the mentoring sessions listening to all the complaints that the mentee has. He needs to share with her the impact that her ranting and raving are having on her colleagues, but he hasn't been successful because she knows that she is right and everyone else is wrong—even her mentor.

As you read this, you are probably considering where your mentee or prospective protégé fits. Besides your mentee, you need to think about where in these four categories you may fall. You may see some of yourself in each category, but try to determine your predominant style. To help, here are some statements to which you can answer yes or no to evaluate yourself.

- I'm known for being cooperative.
- I leave the specific plans to others.
- I dislike working alone.
- I like to prioritize my work and work according to my plan.
- I enjoy being a part of a group.
- I will bring my work home to get it done.
- I am not comfortable in periods of change.
- I am always ready to assume more responsibility.
- I prefer to leave the details to others.
- I don't think I have enough authority.
- I like to prevent or solve problems.
- I am very critical of others.
- I'm known as someone who will bend the rules to reach my goal.
- I believe in following the rules.

Are you primarily task-oriented, a conceptualizer, a visionary, or a socializer? Now, using the same statements, determine in which category your mentee belongs. Does the individual have a reputation for being difficult to work with? Does she prefer to leave the details to others? Does he think he doesn't have enough authority? Not only will this process give you insights into how to work more productively with the other person, but it should also give you insights into how to minimize the likelihood of future conflicts between you and your mentee.

Let's assume that you are a visionary but your mentee is a conceptualizer. You may want to learn to speak your mentee's language, offering feedback in broad outline rather than detail. Let's assume that you are task-oriented and your mentee is a socializer. You may both find it difficult to work together, but should you both lay down your guard, each of you could come away from the relationship with new skills and abilities. You might gain some of the social skills that your mentee already possesses, and your mentee would develop more appreciation of facts and figures, which could be what is keeping your mentee in his or her current position.

What if you are task-oriented and your mentee is predominantly a visionary? You may need to consider more frequent meetings to review goals and get agreement on how each goal will be reached by setting up action plans in concert. Where you expect your mentee to experience problems, raise the issues and work together to identify solutions.

These actions may help. These suggestions won't guarantee to end the personality conflicts you currently have with a mentee, but give them a chance before you walk away from the relationship.

- *Be introspective.* Each time a conflict arises, you need to ask this very important question: How am I contributing to the personality conflict? For instance, a mentor who is always in a hurry may frustrate and even alienate a mentee who needs time to question a manager about some work that needs to be done before meeting with the mentor. A mentee with an untidy workstation may be seen by you, a task-oriented mentor, as disorderly while in reality your mentee may be a visionary and a top performer. Learn to ignore the messy desk and focus on how to use your mentee's sharp mind in a leadership position.
- *Accentuate the positive.* If the individual is making an effort to cooperate with you, despite differences in outlook, demonstrate your appreciation of the effort. Let your mentee know that you both come from very different perspectives and you will work to close the gap, just as your mentee is doing.
- *Talk with the individual.* Talk in a frank but nonthreatening manner, using the "I message" approach or influencing strategy described above.
- *Agree to disagree.* In some mentoring relationships, this may work. Put aside your differences and focus on the development goals you set at the beginning of the relationship. Just as talking out the problem may reveal that your mentee doesn't know that his or her behavior is making you uncomfortable, or that you don't know something you are doing bothers your mentee, agreeing to disagree may likewise get you past the personality conflict. In focusing on the relationship, you and your mentee may create a productive partnership that overrides any personality differences.

As you can see, my intention in helping you to address these difficult situations is to teach you to approach them from a problem-solving mind-set. Learn to look at the situation from both your own perspective and that of your mentee before you decide to walk away from the relationship. This is especially true in special relationships. In Chapter 14, we will talk about these special situations. Here, let me just review some of the problems that you may encounter.

SPECIAL SITUATIONS

A Supervisory Mentor

In this instance, you chose to take on as mentee one of your most talented staff members. Unfortunately, it has prompted jealousy from other staff members who think you are showing this talented individual favoritism. It has made it uncomfortable for your staff mentee. Your staff has become less willing to take on added assignments as they see the best tasks going to your mentee.

What can you do? In this instance, you may want to formalize the program within your department. Announce that each year those staff members with the best performance appraisals will have the opportunity to learn new and exciting skills under your direction. Don't limit your mentorship to a single staff member but to all those who qualify. If you have a 1 to 5 rating system, you might give the added attention to those who regularly score 4—you don't have to require staff members to walk on water to qualify for the extra management coaching.

A Romantic Involvement

You are a female mentor and you chose a young man as mentee, but he seems to misunderstand the reason for his selection. You think he may even have been bragging, and that bragging is behind the office gossip about you both. It's time to make the relationship clear if it wasn't clear at first. Sit the young man down and be very clear about your intentions. Let your mentee know that you see the relationship as strictly professional and that you do not have any social or romantic intentions. Let the gossips know that you see the relationship as strictly professional, and that you do not have any social or romantic intentions. Formalizing the relationship will also help. For instance, meet in your office with the door open to discuss your mentee's progress on the goals set during the previous meeting. This may be an appropriate time to prepare a written agreement that specifies the development goals for your mentee. Set down development goals.

Your reputation is not something you should risk.

If your mentee steps over the line and you feel uncomfortable about it, address the problem right away. Talk about your concerns, and if you and your mentee cannot reach an agreement, or if the problem persists, end the relationship. [Incidentally, the same advice applies if you are the mentee in a mentorship. As I mentioned, you may find yourself being mentored by someone who has a position a level or two above you in mahogany row. Always meet in a public place, such as the office or a restaurant, rather than in a hotel. If your mentor has a reputation as a lothario, don't even pursue the opportunity. If you enter into a mentoring relationship, and your mentor is interested in more than your career, end the relationship. Visit the Human Resources department as well, to protect your position within the organization.]

Cultural Differences

Mentoring partnerships between people from different cultures can present a challenge, because people from different cultures have different traditions, customs, and practices. Therefore, if you do not understand another person's culture, there is greater likelihood of misunderstanding or miscommunication. In addition, some people hold stereotypes of different cultures—they have preconceived notions of how people from different cultures behave which can be a block to truly understanding your mentee.

The solution is to do your research about your new mentee's culture so you have some familiarity with it. Try to step into that person's shoes and understand his or her life. Ask questions. When you are not sure of how to interpret something that has been said, ask what was meant.

Open your mind and be willing to learn not only about the skills, abilities, and knowledge that your mentee brings to the relationship but the cultural differences as well.

A Female or Minority Mentor

Women and people of color face special challenges to getting ahead. Consequently, companies increasingly are developing mentoring programs that offer access to women and other minority members as mentors. (See Chapter 14.) Let's assume that your organization doesn't have such a program, and you, a woman executive, are now mentoring a talented young black woman. You have a good relationship but the young woman has a chip on her shoulder that makes it awkward to give her some development opportunities. She resents the fact that the organization has so few black women in management positions. You work for a stock brokerage that is locked in a time long gone, and your mentee is very much a free spirit whose dreadlocks and bright, flowery agbada robes have generated comments about your selection of the young black woman as your mentee. You have two options: you can ditch her, selecting someone more traditional for your very traditional organization if you want to continue as a mentor, or you can support a movement for a formal mentoring program to help women—of all races—attain positions of management.

It's your choice, reader.

C a s e   S t u d y

JP MORGAN GROWS LEADERS

JP Morgan Partners, the New York City–based investment company, launched its mentoring program after a series of mergers led to talent loss. The company's leadership took this situation seriously because its investors wanted to know who'll be in management in five years. "We're a long-term investment vehicle, so they want to know if the same team will be in place," according to Julie Casella, senior vice president.

The JP Morgan Partners program is companywide, with one-on-one employee mentoring and three days a year devoted to discussing people issues. The company—and mentees—also evaluate mentors based on their mentees' progress and success, with annual awards for mentor of the year.

As a result of the program, the company reports turnover at approximately 2 percent among those it wants to keep. Competitive firms tend to have 25 to 30 percent turnover. The mentoring program is also credited with helping the firm to recruit because it makes the organization stand out from its competition.

8

SUPERVISOR AS MENTOR

Should someone's mentor also be that person's supervisor? I believe that a supervisor can mentor an employee in the sense that the mentor can give the individual developmental opportunities as a part of a performance management system. However, I have found that it is much more difficult for the traditional mentor-protégé relationship to exist between a supervisor and a staff member, no matter how much the mentee deserves the added attention.

Let's look first at some of the reasons why a traditional mentor-protégé relationship is inappropriate. Afterward, I would like to share with you how you can "mentor" (think "empower") your employees as their supervisor.

MENTOR VERSUS SUPERVISOR

When mentors are also their protégé's supervisor, some problems can arise. The manager may feel that his authority is impinged upon. At the same time, the protégé may feel that her supervisor is more concerned about keeping his protégé on board than helping her develop her capabilities and advance in her career. The protégé may also believe that she deserves her supervisor's loyalty, above and beyond what might exist if there relationship was based on positional power.

Positional power itself may be a problem in a mentor-protégé relationship. The supervisor/mentor may guide, suggest, or coach but shouldn't be using power to direct actions.

The roles of mentor and supervisor also differ. The supervisor is responsible for managing the on-the-job performance of staff, including mentors when they are staff members. In the traditional mentoring relationship, a mentor is not involved in performance assessments or appraisals. Likewise, a supervisor's perspective is on the meeting of short-term goals and day-to-day work whereas a mentor will usually have a longer-term, more strategic focus on the protégé's development.

Finally, a mentor doesn't have a vested interest in a protégé's progress whereas a supervisor will be much more subjective.

This may explain why structured mentoring programs make a major effort to skip a level or go across corporate boundaries to find mentors for those who want such assistance. The latter is worthy of mention, particularly in organizations with distinct, sometimes competing functional or geographical corporate cultures.

If we assume that mentoring relationships between those within the same area of an organization too often wind up as "how-to" coaching sessions rather than meetings on personal development, then there is a serious reason why individuals within the same operation should not work together as mentor and protégé. Also, when same-function mentoring relationships are likely, the (unhealthy) element of competition can creep in, whereas taking mentors and protégés from different functions reduces the power and status undertones sometimes present in the mentoring relationship. If I'm a bright young marketing manager and my mentor is a senior VP in marketing, there's going to be an implied status differential that will never fully disappear. I will be thinking about how I can use that relationship to advance in his operation. On the other hand, if I'm a bright young marketing manager and my mentor heads up product development, the relationship is likely to be less status/power based, more development-oriented.

Maybe, most important, when mentor and protégé come from different parts of the organization, there may be a bigger benefit in that the walls between operations may crumble.

SUPERVISORS' ATTITUDES ABOUT MENTORING

Often, supervisors feel threatened when an employee joins a formal mentoring program. Bosses who are not good at developing employees may also not understand the nature of the protégé's development activities. They may be suspicious and resentful of an employee taking time to go to a meeting that is seemingly unrelated to the protégé's current assignment, not understanding that the purpose of attendance is to grow professionally. A boss with this perception of mentoring activities is also overlooking the fact that the skill-building taking place may benefit the protégé's regular job performance as well.

Jealousy is another problem. Often, the protégé's mentor is at a higher level in the organization than the manager. Suddenly, the employee has access to information and networks that the manager lacks. The boss begins to feel inadequate or left out.

Consultants and coaches report that supervisors have sabotaged mentor relationships in those cases where they have felt threatened or isolated from the mentoring process. What can mentors do when such a situation arises?

OVERCOMING OBJECTIONS AND GAINING COMMITMENT

To begin with, mentors can involve the supervisors in the mentoring initiatives from the beginning. When an employee has sought out a mentor and such information is known to the employee's manager, the mentor should be alert to how the new relationship with the employee may affect the relationship with the supervisor. Let me tell you the story of the predicament one mentor found himself in.

Larry heads up public relations in a major manufacturing firm. A talented junior marketer had worked with him on a project. They worked well together, and soon Paula was visiting Larry to discuss some less political and more career-oriented issues with him. Larry was flattered and willingly assumed the role of advisor (think "mentor"). One day, Paula came to the office very upset. Her performance appraisal with her manager, Manny, had gone poorly.

As Larry listened to Paula's complaints, he realized how he had inadvertently contributed to some of her problems. He had asked her assistance on several projects that had taken her away from her day-to-day assignments. Paula had learned a lot from the experience, but, the truth was, the assignments that Manny had expected her to complete hadn't been done on schedule.

It would have been easy for Larry to blame the problem on Paula. She had never told him about these tasks. On the other hand, the work that he had given her was far more interesting than the humdrum tasks that Manny had laid out for his newest hire. Still, he should have asked her about her schedule and her availability to assume additional work to help him, even if he truly needed her assistance and the project would be a learning opportunity for any junior marketing manager.

Larry decided to step in—to talk to Manny about his role—to help Paula. His mentoring relationship with Paula came as a major surprise to Manny. "I see no reason why I should ignore her blatant disregard of deadlines." He continued, "Nor should I forgive you for putting your big foot into my relationship with one of my staff members."

Larry tried to explain how Paula had productively used her time—which meant little to Manny given the lost time on his own work and the costs associated with it. "So, I'm supposed to forgive and forget," he said. "No way."

Larry's situation was awkward because he had an informal relationship with Manny's employee. A structured program is more likely to avoid such difficulty, particularly if supervisors of program participants are involved in the program from the beginning, if possible in the planning stages through focus group participation.

Once a formal plan is completed, supervisors of potential protégés can also participate in briefing meetings and ask questions to better understand the process. One milestone of the program may be a meeting between the mentor and supervisor once the protégé/employee has selected the mentor.

Depending on the interest of supervisors in the mentoring efforts, they may also be invited to follow up mentoring meetings and in ongoing evaluations of the program. Individuals in charge of the corporate initiative should encourage mentors to liaise regularly with their employees' mentors. Ideally, employees should feel comfortable enough to discuss generally how the relationship between them and their mentors is going. They need not break confidentiality about the efforts themselves but they should be able to discuss the mentoring effort they are receiving and any special skill and experience development.

The kind of interaction that can reduce a boss's concern about the protégé's special relationship with another, perhaps higher-level manager is encouraged at Merrill Lynch. The mentor is encouraged to call each of his protégés' managers and get acquainted. Mentors are encouraged to work with four protégés during a six-month period, and both the mentor and the protégés keep the managers apprised of what they're doing.

The point of such efforts is to avoid a situation like Paula's and instead to have the full and active support of supervisors and managers outside the mentor relationship. A positive experience with mentoring can encourage a supervisor to become a mentor of someone who is not a staff member. Indeed, in time, the boss may learn that his job can be made easier when the protégé is taking full responsibility for the tasks of preparing and executing a development plan. And the feedback that the mentor gives the protégé transfers to his day-to-day job. A savvy supervisor can reinforce this behavior by commending the employee for taking the initiative in performance development, thereby demonstrating to the higher-level mentor his own supervisory skills.

Finally, a supervisor who is new to the position can benefit from observing how a competent mentor interacts with the protégé. The boss doesn't have to admit to a managerial shortcoming, but she can watch the mentor and protégé and then imitate a talented mentor in performance planning and feedback discussions not only with the protégé but with other staff members. A manager told me, "I'm doing a much better supervisory job with my direct reports by applying the strategies I learned from my mentor's coaching of me and observing him coach one of my staff members."

Are there occasions when a supervisor can mentor one of his own reports? Yes, as part of performance management, supervisors can assume a quasi-mentoring role, empowering their top performers. This isn't the same as true mentoring but it gives professional growth opportunities to those employees fortunate enough to have the added attention of their supervisors.

Let me explain.

THE ROLE OF SUPERVISORS TO MENTEES

A supervisor performs three developmental roles with employees. Monthly coaching is conducted to assess the need for training or further direction to get day-to-day work done. This form of coaching is very similar to the coaching in a mentoring situation but the intent is to identify performance difficulties before they call for counseling, which is an either-or process—either the employee turns around her performance or the employee is terminated.

Counseling is very similar to coaching in that it is a one-on-one discussion between the employee and the supervisor for the purpose of identifying the cause of the problem performance and then developing an action plan to turn around the behavior. Generally, termination follows no improvement or repetition of a chronic performance problem.

The third and final phase of this performance management approach is empowerment or departmental mentoring during which the manager offers coaching to increase the high-potential's employability by giving her more opportunity to learn, to be recognized, and to increase visibility within the organization.

The manager's goal by words and actions is to send a clear message to the employee that she is respected. In many instances, the supervisor shares leadership with the mentored or empowered employee. The employee is encouraged to view problems as opportunities and to come to the manager with new methods of doing things.

If you decide to become a mentor to a staff member, you must be willing to make a commitment to do more than coach and counsel—you have to empower the individual. Start by asking yourself the following questions:

- What areas of responsibility do I currently have that I would most like to see handled by someone else?
- What skills does one of my employees have that are being underused?
- How could I better use my time if I were freed of some of the hands-on managing I do now?

Chances are, the answers to these three questions alone can get you started thinking about how empowering a key staff member can improve your department and help advance the employee professionally.

Remember, however, declaring an employee ready to be empowered or to be mentored is easy. Actually getting the individual to accept the role can be difficult. Workers often look cynically on the offer to explore opportunities for streamlining procedures, to have a voice in decisions, or to otherwise take on the manager's role, such as leading a task team.

It is natural for employees to be reluctant to make suggestions for change, but in a positive work environment—one in which the supervisor demonstrates daily a willingness to share leadership—the supervisor can train key employees to do so. The key is to meet resistance with patient persistence.

Unless you gain an employee's trust, quasi-mentoring of staff won't work. Those employees you wish to treat like protégés must feel free to share their concerns and needs with you as they would with a traditional mentor.

So it is important that you have the respect of your work team—certainly, that individual you wish to truly empower. Toward that, you want to provide a positive work environment. That means not only demonstrating that you are credible—for instance, when you promise something, you deliver—but also creating a work environment in which your staff protégés have an opportunity to develop skills that go beyond those they have today. You need to work with them to help them develop these—both the decision-making and the job skills they will need to become a productive part of their company's value chain. You need to communicate clearly the message that, as staff protégés take on new responsibilities, mistakes will occur but that they will learn from these mistakes. The whole organization will profit as its human assets grow in value from the capability of individual members taking on ever-challenging projects and tasks with minimal supervision.

As staff mentor, you give truth to the talk of shared goals and leadership by allowing your most talented staff members to step out of their boxes and demonstrate in a supportive environment the talents and creativity you have helped them develop. By allowing employees a more active role in problem solving, you increase your quasi-mentees with feelings of satisfaction with their jobs while freeing yourself to devote attention to planning or other managerial tasks.

The foundations are laid for employees to resolve problems on their own when you include staff in goal setting and development of action plans. If staff members are to address their own problems they encounter as they do their work, they need that information. It helps them to make the right decisions and focus their energy where it helps them to make the decisions that offer the greatest return for the organization. But tapping into a mission or goals isn't always sufficient. Nor do bromides about the value of employee initiative constitute a supportive environment for out-of-the-box thinking for staff members.

Yes, there is a risk associated with granting employees the freedom to take initiative. But you should not be risk-averse. You need to recognize that increasing employees' freedom over their work may have costly and tumultuous repercussions, but it also may prepare staff to be more productive and bring clearer insights to problems as a result of their proximity to them. And you should help to minimize the risks by training and the placement of control systems that allow you to stay abreast of employee actions.

You can minimize the risk by:

- *Keeping all lines of communication open.* By holding biweekly or monthly meetings with staff protégés, you stay familiar with employee actions. Likewise, you share information with these empowered employees— even if you think they don't need that information to do their jobs. The more these employees know about company events, deadlines, difficulties with suppliers, and the like, the better equipped they are to make intelligent decisions when problems arise.
- *Listening.* Joe has been complaining for some time about the location of so many foreign subsidiaries in his territory. His supervisor never really heard his complaints. Consequently, she never met with him to develop specific action plans to help him make up for lost sales from his region. If you worry that you may not have sufficient time to hear out all ideas, in some instances you may want to have an employee check with you before implementing a plan.
- *Giving frequent, objective, and initiative-encouraging feedback.* Even when a problem arises from your employees' use of their initiative, you don't

want to dwell so much on the dilemma that you discourage further risk taking by the employees. They need to be coached specifically on what they did wrong and what they did right, and coached, in general, on how to solve problems.

- *Conducting ongoing training where it is evidently needed.* If an employee makes a mistake in solving a problem, and it is likely that that problem might be encountered again, then you might want to have the person undergo training in that part of the solution where she is weak. Say you have someone who suddenly found herself required to set terms with a representative for another firm for purchase of her firm's services. The person did a bad negotiating job, so you might want to have that individual undergo some training in negotiation for the next time the problem crops up. Perhaps you suggest that there is a point in problem solving where she needs to bring you into the negotiation; then she can observe and learn from your negotiation style (think "shadowing") and determine what terms represent a win-win situation for both firms.

If the rapport exists, the supervisors become mentors to their staff members. After all, consider that a mentor helps an employee:

- Set long-term goals and short-term objectives
- Explore new directions to achieve goals
- Identify personal strengths and weaknesses
- Find ways to develop and grow

Many of these tasks take place during your employees' performance assessments. Should you wish to extend your assistance to high achievers, you need to commit yourself to devoting more coaching time, sometimes even helping your high achievers identify and discard limiting beliefs.

WORKING WITH HIGH ACHIEVERS

Beth is a high achiever. She is hard working and very capable in her work. Though it is hard to believe, Beth lacks self-confidence. Her manager decided to mentor her, and one of his first goals in working with her was to defuse this limiting belief that kept her from fully utilizing her potential. It wasn't easy to do. Hank, her boss, never could determine the source of the belief. We often acquire these limiting beliefs as youngsters. Maybe a family member or a teacher told you that you weren't good with numbers. The idea took hold, and subsequently you believe you can't add two and two together.

In Beth's case, sometime in her life, someone made her feel awkward and insecure, and that idea stuck. Consequently, she had rejected every opportunity to lead a team of coworkers on a project. Hank had watched the teams, as team sponsor (think "team mentor," see Chapter 10), and he could see how she often took the lead in discussions and in coming up with ideas and planning how to implement them. Yet, each time he asked her to head up a team, she refused. "I am just not leadership material," she would tell him.

Hank sat down with her during her next performance review and he discussed her leadership potential. He realized that he had to help her see how competent she really was. Hank couldn't help but think, "I have so many staff members who come into an appraisal meeting ready to prove how much they have earned a high rating for the year, and Beth sits in a meeting and tells me how she could have done more and better despite the fact that she has outdone her coworkers in almost every assignment."

To help her realize her leadership potential, he had her list all her accomplishments as she sat before him. At first, he had to coax her to list some tasks she had completed. After a while, her pen raced across the paper. A smile appeared on her face. "Do you see why I think you have the potential to lead a project team?" Hank asked.

He pointed out how many of the ideas of past teams in which she participated came from her. He also told of his observations of her in team interaction, and how she naturally gained the attention of her peers. Beth decided to give it a try. Hank promised to be present in case a problem arose. Beth was unsure and raced through her opening remarks, but as she gained confidence in her leadership skills, the team moved forward.

Beth realized she had succeeded as she saw Hank quietly get up from his chair at the back of the room and leave, confident that she was in charge.

That wasn't the last change with which Hank helped Beth. He knew her well, and he felt that she had great ideas, but she didn't always get the credit she deserved. She was so passionate about her opinions that she spoke too quickly. Her peers knew her well enough to hear her out and follow her direction. Those from other parts of the organization, however, became defensive when she shared her ideas with them. So Hank had to not only teach Beth that she had leadership capability but also demonstrate her value to those outside of the department. This wasn't so easy, but fortunately Beth trusted Hank—a critical element when supervisors mentor employees—and consequently welcomed his feedback.

Hank could have told Beth what to do and coached her to ensure that she practiced what he preached. Instead, he decided to make her aware of this shortcoming on her own. He included her in a discussion group that would be filmed for the staff. Beth made a number of good points, but her tendency to speak too fast and loudly to get attention was evident on the tape—and evident to Beth. Her peers didn't say anything—after all, they knew Beth's style. But Beth was smart enough to see that she lost the attention of several members in the room when she became passionate about an issue.

After viewing the film, Beth sought Hank. "Hank," she asked, "do you know of any course that could improve my presentation skills?" "Sure," he said, picking up a brochure he curiously had right on his desk. "I sent one of my former staff members to that course there," he said, pointing to the communications program, "because he felt he needed to polish his presentation skills."

"Well," Beth told Hank, "I think I could benefit from improving my interpersonal communication and presentation skills, too," Beth said.

Attendance at the course made Beth aware of some tricks to control her enthusiasm that professional speakers used. Consequently, another of Beth's shortcomings was eliminated.

Hank's efforts wound up losing him a very talented staff member. She was promoted to head up a division of the company in another state. He's still her advisor, coach, broker, and advocate but long-distance, via e-mail and cell phone.

Hank continues to mentor staff members, despite the fact that he lost Beth as a consequence. He has found it worth the effort because he had two years of Beth's time during which she took over a large portion of his work, freeing him to explore new opportunities for the division and thereby increasing the bottom line.

What can we learn from Hank's style of mentoring his staff members?

- *Don't tell, empower.* Resist the temptation to tell a staff member with more potential than his current job demands what to do. Rather, allow the individual to think through the problem and come up with solutions independently.
- *Focus on the staff member, not the problem.* When your quasi-protégé approaches you with a problem, you might be tempted to solve it. By doing so, however, you will be denying the individual a valuable learning opportunity. Concentrate instead on the staff member's professional development. By listening to your staff member, like Hank listened to Beth about her lack of self-confidence, he better understood her fears. From this, he was able to gain insights into those areas in which Beth needed to grow.
- *Offer guidance, not solutions.* Yes, Hank knew that Beth should take that course on interpersonal communications, and he was ready with the

brochure when she needed it. But he left it to Beth to discover her need to improve her communication skills. When he made a suggestion, instead of saying, "you should," he shared his own experience or that of another staff member who had had a similar problem. Then he asked Beth if the same solution might work for her. Another way to offer help without providing the answers is to play the role of devil's advocate. This approach helps staff members see the consequence of their decisions. The idea is that the more a manager encourages staff members to develop solutions, the greater their growth and the more likely that empowerment will occur.

While it is better for a supervisor, serving as mentor, to let staff mentees come up with their own solutions, there are times when direct reports require advice from their supervisory mentor. Also, there were occasions in Hank's career when he found he had to direct some mentees that needed help in finding the answers. This was especially true when he had new hires with high potential. But Hank also realized that the frequency with which he told staff members the answers would impact their development—actually, the more times he told them, the slower their professional growth. In essence, Hank realized that the secret to mentoring his staff was to gain their trust and understand their needs. There is no right way to behave in every situation, but what is appropriate in each supervisory/mentor-employee/mentee relationship is that you make a conscious choice about what will be best for your direct report's development.

Because Hank believed in coaching, counseling, and mentoring, he was able to follow up with those employees to which he offered a little extra coaching to determine the outcome. It wasn't just that Beth improved her interpersonal skills, or that another staff member, Jackie, took on purchasing responsibilities for the office, or that Kwame showed he could work well with customers, but that Beth, Jackie, Kwame, and the many others that Hank mentored grew and developed professionally.

There's one last issue to address if you wish to mentor one of your staff members: Which one?

DEFINING HIGH ACHIEVERS

You may want to mentor a staff member but fear jealousy may arise if the individual you choose isn't seen by peers as a top performer. Fortunately, high achievers—potential mentees on your staff—can be identified by their behavior. As you consider whether you want to mentor a staff member, consider these traits among high achievers to see if you have a candidate on staff.

- *High achievers use their talents.* Those staff members who succeed in extraordinary ways are those who have found the few unique talents they possess and use them to maximum benefit. Talent, however, isn't enough.
- *High achievers work hard.* Some of these hard workers may have average talent but they work really hard. Working hard doesn't necessarily mean putting in long hours, although passion for one's work is important. But working hard also means working smart—setting goals and obtaining results, whether that takes one hour or 50. That means understanding what's required of the job at hand, sticking to it when others are goofing off, and keeping an open and curious mind.
- *High achievers are optimistic.* The staff members you are seeking have a can-do attitude, as least in the field they've chosen to excel in. When you're optimistic, you latch on to opportunities in a situation and use them to your advantage. You don't want to focus on the pessimists on staff. They are blind to the opportunities and they use their dour attitude about a situation to avoid acting.
- *High achievers expect much.* Journalist/philosopher Sydney Harris once said, "Those who expect a lot out of life seem to get it."
- *High achievers include others.* They are the team leaders and team players. They recognize that they can only do so much on their own. They realize that they'll achieve more, faster, if they get work done with and through others. [This was the innate ability that set Beth apart from her peers in Hank's view.]
- *High achievers remain unflappable.* Achievers take setbacks in stride. They don't let obstacles deter them from their objective. In a crisis, they actually are calmer—you never see them sweat. Their demeanor inspires confidence and followership.
- *High achievers don't compromise.* Those with the potential for success set their sights high and don't settle for less than that for which they aim. They know they may have to give a little to get what they want, but they don't compromise on the big things.
- *High achievers focus on the positive.* Dale Carnegie said it best, "Don't criticize, condemn, or complain." He clearly was right. After all, it rarely does any good. For another, you're identifying your own weaknesses. Complainers tell the world that they aren't capable of accomplishing something.

- *High achievers act.* Yes, they are the doers. They don't sit back and wait for things to happen in their favor. They are the workers.
- *High achievers take responsibility.* I have become a fan of Donald Trump's TV show *The Apprentice.* I know it doesn't come that close to real life in business, but I find the contestants' response to Trump's critiques of interest, as well as his own remarks. Repeatedly, I have heard Trump and his team of advisors point out the importance of accepting responsibility for your decisions. The best way to avoid being "fired" is to accept accountability for your actions, even if they are the wrong ones.

Train Mentees to Think Critically

Declaring employees to be empowered is easy, but actually getting them to accept ownership of their work processes can be difficult. Even if you offer to mentor a staff member, the person may reject the opportunity. Workers have come to look cynically on corporate promises encouraging them to do more with the promise of opportunity for greater employability and professional advancement.

Demonstrate that you mean it. Show that established procedures are not sacred so that your employees can explore opportunities to improve efficiency and quality with confidence.

It is natural for a staff member to be reluctant to accept your offer to help professionally, but in a positive work environment, you can gradually convince the individual that you mean what you say. Begin the process by defining the operating terms. Otherwise, the lucky employee might be uncertain what is happening. At the very least:

- *Turn employees' questions back to them.* Don't be so quick to offer a solution to a problem, even when it's obvious to you. Ask the individual, "What do you think you should do?" Then listen to the answer and avoid commenting until the employee is finished. You may need to ask some follow-up questions in order to get the employee to think of a solution independently.
- *Encourage employees to consult coworkers.* Instead of providing answers, suggest that your employees ask for advice from coworkers who may have had to deal with the same situation. You may at first have to ask the coworker to help the employee, but eventually it will help the group to work more cooperatively as a team and help your staff mentee grow in the job.

(continued)

- *Meet resistance with patient persistence.* There will be high achievers who are perfectly happy with the status quo and have little or no interest in the opportunity you are offering. They may prefer to put in an honest day's work and go home and forget about it until the next morning. However, with some persistence it is possible to win over these individuals to accept your offer of mentorship and take on more accountability. You can encourage likely candidates by focusing on what they do best and asking for help from them when needed.

9

TRAPS TO AVOID

I wish I could say that once you define your responsibilities and those of your protégé or mentee, there are no problems other than those that will arise as you coach, broker, and serve as advocate for your mentee. Unfortunately, this isn't so. There are problems that you may encounter—some of your own making.

First, let's look at problems that seem improbable, but which mentors tell me they have encountered.

OOPS! DID I REALLY DO THAT?

Let's consider what my good friend Charlie did. His best friend's son, Mark, needed advice about setting up a real estate firm. Charlie heads up a major business in the industry, and Mark's dad went to Charlie and asked if he could spend some time with his boy. Charlie agreed and shared his own experiences, which included the difficulties he encountered when he started out. His story was so discouraging that Mark decided to go into another line of business—to open up a restaurant. He enjoyed cooking and felt he could manage a restaurant if he had the capital to finance the business.

I don't need to tell you the rest of the story. Mark's dad put money into his son's idea and so did Charlie. He told me afterward, "I felt obligated to do so—after all, I had discouraged his initial career goal." What happened? It changed Charlie's relationship with Mark! No longer could Charlie be objective. In essence, there was a conflict of interest. He couldn't be neutral any longer about his relationship with Mark. Nor could Mark be objective about Charlie's feedback. Actually, the restaurant did well after a few rocky months, but during that interim period, Charlie continued to offer constructive feedback.

The problem was that Charlie knew little about the restaurant business and much of his advice ran counter to advice Mark got from other restaurant owners, though Mark felt obligated to accept Charlie's advice. Mark worried that Charlie would no longer offer feedback and would withdraw his financial support, which he still desperately needed.

What should Charlie have done? When Mark became discouraged, Charlie could have sat down with him and shared the positive aspects of a career in real estate instead of focusing only the tough side. Further, he could have volunteered to be there to offer advice, although he would have to have reminded Mark that he would be facing considerable competition, including the firm for which Charlie himself worked.

If Charlie felt he couldn't offer objective advice given the competitive situation, he could have recommended as a mentor for Mark someone else, perhaps a former employee who was now retired.

If Mark had chosen to go into the restaurant business regardless of his subsequent discussion with Charlie, and then had asked Charlie if he would like to be an investor, Charlie should have answered as follows: "I'm pleased to be asked but I have to say no. I'd like to keep our relationship strictly a mentoring one at this time. In time, you may want to seek out someone with experience in running a restaurant. At that time, our relationship as mentor and mentee will have changed. At that point, I'd be glad to discuss other options, like investing in the business. Right now, let's see if we can identify some other financial resources you can turn to."

ROLE REVERSAL

Let me share with you another awkward situation that a mentor found herself in.

Earlier in the book, I mentioned that you may mentor someone who is on another career track and, due to organizational shifts, actually winds up in a position above you on the corporate career ladder. The good news about such situations is that, based on your past positive relationship, that mentee is likely to use her position to help you to rise in your own career. This works well for both you and your protégé. Your mentee returns the help you offered, and you earn the position you probably deserved all along but didn't get because of lack of visibility. What you don't want is to find yourself working for your former mentee—which is what happened to my friend, Rosemary.

Rosemary had mentored Scott when he was an assistant marketing manager and she was VP of marketing. When the company downsized, Rosemary found herself one of those laid off. Scott stayed, was given the title of marketing manager, and assumed many of Rosemary's former responsibilities. Rosemary decided to set herself up as an independent consultant, and her firm was beginning to show a profit when she got a call from Scott. The downturn was still serious at the company, but he had been given approval to hire someone to assist on one or two marketing campaigns. He wanted to reciprocate for all the former advice he had received from her by offering her the assignment.

What Rosemary should have said was: "No, thank you. I appreciate your faith in my ability. However, I have several clients that demand almost all of my attention. If I can give you feedback on any work that is done by an outside service, I'd be delighted to do so, but otherwise I have to refuse." Instead, Rosemary said yes.

As a consequence, Rosemary found herself at Scott's beck and call. He rejected almost all of her ideas, and he often quoted back to her advice she couldn't help but wonder if she had given to him when she had been his mentor. She hated coming into the office and being told to wait until Scott was free, and then sit in her former office and present her ideas to Scott.

To this day, Rosemary isn't certain whether it was her own response to the fact that she was now doing work that Scott had done as her mentee that made it difficult for her to work with him or if Scott was on a power trip and liked to make his former mentor jump at his commands. Whatever the reason, after several months, Rosemary called Scott and suggested he find someone else to work for the company. She also recommended some up-and-coming firms that might be acceptable.

The moral: Unless it's a matter of starvation, don't work for your mentee.

PERSONAL COUNSELOR

Another trap that mentors can fall into is becoming so wrapped up in a mentee's life that they lose perspective about their role.

Jim was mentoring Steve, helping him successfully manage a new product project. He had offered Steve several suggestions to move ahead with the project but it seemed as if Steve had done nothing over the previous week.

When Jim asked why, Steve admitted that he was having marital problems. His wife had left him. She had evidence of his infidelity.

When Jim told me the story, he admitted that he had been tempted to offer advice based on his own happy family life. "Fortunately, I didn't, however," he said. "That isn't the advice and counsel I promised to provide Steve. He needed to see a family counselor and that's the only advice on his personal situation I gave him. I, then, returned to the discussion of the project and what he should do next."

If a mentee is experiencing family difficulties, drug or alcohol misuse, depression, or other potentially complex and even life-threatening situations, then he needs to seek the help of a psychologist or personal counselor. If a mentee reveals a personal issue beyond the mentor's capabilities, the best response the mentor can make is, "I care very much about you and want to support you as you deal with this. As we discussed when we set up our relationship, we may run into some issues about which I'm not an authority. I believe this is one of those situations. Can we discuss available services within the community that can help you?"

Jim took the same approach that a manager would take in conducting a counseling session with an employee that announced he had a drug addiction, sick child, or other personal problem. He recommended that Steve seek professional help but pointed to the importance for Steve to succeed in his work as well. This approach is applicable if the mentoring relationship is an informal one or a part of a formal program.

THE WRONG PAIR

Another trap that you, as a mentor, can fall into is to pair yourself with someone that you don't like. It may be a personality conflict. It may be that you feel that the mentee is too insecure to take the tough criticism that you are known for. It may be that the mentee is too demanding of your time and too dependent on your assistance. Whatever the reason, the relationship is not working out.

What can you do?

The ideal is to avoid the situation before it even happens. Take time at the outset to become acquainted with the mentee. Determine if you have shared values and, more important, similar expectations from the relationship. Such know-how will prevent unwelcome surprises later on.

If you believe that time spent with this individual could be more productively spent with another, equally talented employee who would be more willing to listen to your feedback, it is best to end the mentoring relationship before it has even begun. Let the person know that you want to see him or her advance careerwise, but suggest more suitable candidates as mentor for the person.

Laura, a friend of mine, has been in publishing for over 30 years. Her company has a formal mentoring program, and she found herself matched with Marv, who is in systems. Over breakfast, Laura and I discussed the situation. "Why did they give me Marv to mentor?" she asked me. "How can I help him? He should be mentoring me in systems."

Looking back, it is possible that Laura should have waited before questioning the decision by the program coordinator to pair the two. In truth, both could have learned from each other. Laura had considerable experience in project management, something that Marv seemed to need. In turn, from their association, Laura could have picked up a lot of information about how her firm's systems program worked, information she could have later used when she became publisher. Instead, Laura was assigned a new editorial assistant to mentor. Marv was paired with someone from purchasing.

TOO MUCH PRESSURE

Laura may also have worried about how she might have been viewed if she failed as a mentor. A trap many mentors fall into is the belief that they will be measured by peers based on the performance of their mentees. "People may begin to wonder about my own competence," they tell themselves. Concerned about the mentee, some even worry that rather than help the up-and-comer under their wing, they may hinder development by giving them the wrong direction.

However, most individuals familiar with mentoring recognize that many people contribute to the development of a new or an advancing professional. One mentor will not make the difference between a mentee becoming the next Bill Gates or Carla Fiorina.

THE COMPETITION

What if the mentee is as talented as Bill Gates or Carla Fiorina? Fear that the mentee may take their best secrets and strategies and surpass them is another trap into which some mentors fall. Needless to say, such thinking can be destructive to a mentoring relationship. This is unfortunate because being a mentor can actually set up someone for further advancement. A wise mentor recognizes that as a mentee grows professionally, the mentor can take the lead in redefining the relationship. Such leadership generally ends in a mutually rewarding respect for one another. When the mentor ends the relationship—often passing the mentee on to another—the mentor can do so with justifiable pride in the contribution to the professional development of the next generation of leaders in the organization.

My friend Bill worried about mentoring Lynn because of a fear that some day *soon* she would outperform him. Without question, Lynn was extremely talented, with a natural flair for leading people. But Lynn admired Bill for qualities that she lacked—such as his ability to work with numbers and put together proposals for management approval. I met Lynn once, and it was clear that she was the best press agent Bill could have within the organization. "If I can put together a business plan as well as he does one day," she said, "then I'll know that I have what it takes to make it to the top."

How did I help Bill? Actually, he helped himself. He realized that he had two choices: he could stay where he was or he could move up in the organization. The company had a structured mentoring program and Bill signed up. He was given a senior executive in human resources as his mentor and two years later, he was promoted to business development VP. Lynn is one of his staff members in charge of team planning.

WHEN MENTORING HURTS

What kinds of mentoring problems should cause you to dissolve a relationship? For one, some mentors find that mentoring can inhibit their mentees' development rather than support it. If a talented mentee becomes too dependent on the mentor, there will be a decline in performance. Rather than try to resolve problems on his own, the mentee will continually run to the mentor for help. But, worse, rather than begin to build his own network of contacts, the talented mentee will become dependent on the mentor's network of contacts both within and outside the organization.

Another problem occurs when the mentee becomes so wrapped up in the idea of being part of a mentorship that she won't focus on the assignments that come with the mentorship or, alternatively, may focus more on those assignments and ignore her day-to-day work.

TWO ACHILLES HEELS

Some mentoring relationships fail because the mentor discovers that the mentee lacks the ability to develop the new skills important to his career advancement. It's often not a matter of developing new job skills but rather acquiring political savvy or a better fit with the corporate culture.

That's the mentee's Achilles heel. Mentors also can have an Achilles heel that only becomes evident in the mentoring relationship. These mentors lack the communication or managerial styles critical to mentoring. For instance, the mentor may criticize rather than listen, or may provide the mentee with answers rather than risk that the mentee will make a mistake. Or the mentor may become more than an advocate for the mentee, assuming the role of press agent, perhaps selling the availability of the mentee as a team leader not because the individual is qualified for the task but rather because of the relationship between the mentor and the individual.

PROBLEMS IN UNIQUE MENTORING RELATIONSHIPS

Earlier in the book, I wrote about the increase in cross-gender mentoring and also mentoring by those within the same command chain. Problems can arise in both situations of which you should be aware as a mentor.

Cross-Gender Mentoring

Rumors can arise if you are a male manager and you choose to mentor a female employee or if you are a female manager and choose to mentor a male employee. The likelihood of a sexual relationship between the mentor and mentee can easily become the topic of discussion on the corporate grapevine, regardless of the parties' personal or professional reputation. One manager was warned by his boss that he might not get a promotion he clearly had earned because of his mentoring relationship with a female staff member, despite her fine professional reputation. The office rumor mill said that he was spending so much time with the young woman that they must be having an affair—which they weren't.

The manager was happily married. The young woman wasn't married but she had a boyfriend. Their meetings were always in his office. Neither had ever been the source of office gossip in the past. Yet the manager had to choose between continuing to help his assistant achieve her goal of becoming a CPA or ensuring his promotion.

I wish I could say that this was a unique situation, unlikely to happen to other mixed gender mentoring relationships. Unfortunately, that's not so. The press contacted me on this very issue not so long ago. Their question:

Should a female mentee always keep the door open while being counseled by a male mentor? My reply: "No woman should find herself in a mentoring situation with a male in which she feels she has to keep the door open to protect either herself or her reputation." But, in retrospect, that reply was too simplistic.

Cross-gender mentoring is open to misunderstanding in today's sexually conscious world. Those who enter into it need to be prepared for some people, often jealous of the special attention that a mentee may get, to spread rumors. Should you find yourself in such a situation, the good news is that the gossip mongers usually get bored when they see no fire and move on, seeking other signs of smoke elsewhere.

Getting back to the two individuals previously mentioned, despite his boss's warning, the mentor got his promotion even though he continued to help his mentee advance in her career. Rather than give up being a mentor to those in his company, he extended his mentorship to include another staff member—another woman—who took over his job when he moved up. As for his original mentee, she received her degree in accounting, married her boyfriend, and now works for a tax return processing company.

Mentoring Your Subordinate's Subordinate

An equally awkward situation occurs when you decide to mentor a subordinate of one of your direct reports. This happened to my friend Bob. Karen had lots of potential and Bob thought that she could take on several special projects he needed to have done so he spent some coaching time with her. But Karen reported to Murdock, Bob's direct report, and he recognized that Murdock might be upset if he learned that Karen was being mentored by his boss without his knowledge.

Bob didn't think that Murdock would object, so he was surprised when he did. Actually, Murdock offered to take on the projects himself. "I can oversee the work," he said. "I'll assign the actual work to Karen and other staff members," he explained. "You and I can get together to discuss progress weekly," Murdock told Bob.

Bob didn't know what to say. It would take care of the projects, but Karen wouldn't get the added attention that he felt would enable the company to benefit from her full potential. So Bob asked Murdock if he would mentor Karen. "No," said Murdock. "I think Karen is essential to the department—a wonderful, conscientious worker with lots of potential—but I see no reason to take up my time with this."

Bob suggested that Murdock and he discuss the matter later in his office. In the meantime, Bob checked Murdock's personnel file. Based on the past evaluations, it was evident that Murdock was energetic and hard working, but he was also a micromanager. No departing employee had kind words for him. All felt that he had a big ego and a great desire to run things his way. "Clearly, this isn't someone who would want me to give attention to his subordinate," Bob thought.

Bob's solution was to keep Murdock in the loop while also finding a way to mentor Karen. Bob suggested that he and Murdock mentor Karen together. They would meet weekly to review Karen's progress. By involving Murdock, Bob would minimize any feeling that Murdock might have that he was losing control over his own direct report. These weekly meetings would also give Bob the chance to see if the added attention he planned to give Karen created work problems for her—from Murdock.

Bob felt justified in mentoring Karen but he was wise enough to realize that problems might occur between Murdock and Karen—and he acted accordingly.

REMEDIAL PROBLEMS

So far, we've discussed problems that might cause you to dissolve a mentoring relationship or that might create problems outside the relationship. Now let's look at some mentoring problems that can be successfully addressed.

Failure to Live Up to Expectations

You may have selected within the organization a top performer whom you thought you could advance professionally, but the person hasn't lived up to your expectations. The potential may still be evident to you, but the mentee hasn't been adhering to any of the suggestions you have made. The mentee might have misunderstood your offer to be available to provide feedback, or to broker, or to serve as an advocate; instead, she might have interpreted it as a fast track to advancement without the need for any further effort on her part to develop the competencies you originally expected of her.

If this is the case, then it is time to make it clear to the individual that the extra effort you are making in the form of mentoring has a price, and that is increased performance, development of new skills or abilities, leadership of a team effort, or whatever development goals on which you both agreed.

You also want to be clear about what you are offering the mentee. Too often, mentees think that they will be getting not only additional professional advice but also protection from organizational pressures, perhaps even a downsizing. The truth is, even if the mentor had the clout, it isn't a part of the deal.

Because such misconceptions can exist, a mentor has to be very specific in discussions with a prospective mentee about what will be provided. This is particularly the situation when mentoring a staff member. The employee shouldn't expect to be favored over other staff members because of the extraordinary relationship.

Incidentally, this issue of expectations goes both ways. Too often, mentors assume that initiating the relationship is the most important part of mentoring. Not so. Sustaining it is the critical part. Expressing one's intention to mentor someone is, at most, only 10 percent of building the partnership; the ongoing communication and support represent the other 90 percent.

When that continuous effort isn't forthcoming, no matter what your assertions about how important the mentee and his career are, the likelihood is that the protégé will become frustrated. He will become disenchanted about the relationship and even doubt his own worth.

Under such circumstances, you have two alternatives. You can seek out someone else to mentor your mentee, perhaps a peer who has more time than you do right now, or you can find the time. Maybe you can meet during lunch; or if your calendar is so busy that you can't meet in your office during the workday, you might suggest that you and the mentee meet either before the day begins or after work.

This is an issue that can arise even if you try conscientiously to find time for your mentee. Some mentees may have an expectation beyond reality about how much availability you are going to give. So it is best to be clear at the beginning about how much time each week or month you can devote to the individual. As you think about how much time you want to give, keep in mind that if you devote too much time to the relationship, the mentee can become too dependent on you. Worse, you both will find yourselves sitting together in the office with nothing to talk about but your mentee's dog or your wife's new job.

If you can, mark your calendar ahead of time to meeting with the mentee to ensure that you always have the agreed-upon time available.

Unrealistic Development Goals

Ask yourself, "Am I asking too much of my mentee?" If your demands for significant improvement in your mentee's performance are excessive, hostility may grow between you and your mentee. Rather than list the accomplishments you expect from your mentee without the mentee's participation, sit down with the individual and work out the list together. The final list will reflect your goals for the individual and also the day-to-day responsibilities, a much more realistic start to the mentoring relationship.

Unfair Treatment by the Mentor

The opposite of a mentor who believes that a mentee can raise the world on his shoulders is a mentor who believes that the mentee can do no right, with the mentee receiving harsher feedback than coworkers do for the same mistakes.

Jack was editor-in-chief of a chain of magazines. One of his staff writers reminded him of himself as a young editor, so he tended to give Jeff more time and attention than some of his other writers. They lunched frequently together which was time Jeff appreciated because Jack often offered to advise the fledgling reporter. When the staff heard that the publisher was looking for a columnist, Jeff felt he had a chance but he also knew that the competition for the position would be tough.

When he learned that Jack was being asked for his opinion, Jeff felt that the odds had improved. After all, Jack had told him over lunch that Steve was always late with copy, Jan didn't know what a good story was, Howard wrote like he was still in high school, and Abe didn't know the industry well enough. Jeff thought he had the job. It came as a surprise when Jan got the job.

Over lunch with Jack, he discovered why. Jack had shared with the publisher all of Jeff's shortcomings but none of those of his coworkers. Why? Jack didn't want to look as if he was showing favoritism. So he didn't talk about Jan's inability to spell, her lateness to the office and, most important, her poor selection of subject matter. Instead, Jack spent his hour with the publisher talking about Jeff's soft leads and willingness to take on more tasks, which explained why the publisher told Jeff that he was so good at his job that he wanted him to assume more responsibility—of course, without pay or promotion.

Jeff told me, "I had considered our discussions confidential, so I was especially upset that Jack had shared with Lincoln the subjects of our conversations over the past year."

Clearly, Jack had violated the confidentiality that is a key to a mentoring relationship. But his fears about being accused of favoritism also caused him to be unfair to the talented superstar on the team. Incidentally, being passed over for promotion prompted Jeff to leave the firm. He became editor of a competitive magazine.

Bottom line: You, as a mentor, may be accused of showing favoritism. The only defense you have is evidence that the person you are mentoring is worthy of the time and talent you give to his or her professional development.

Measuring Your Current Relationship

Reread the list of traps to see if you have inadvertently fallen into one. Then ask yourself these ten questions about your mentoring relationship to be sure that you and your mentee have no misunderstandings and that you, the mentee, and your organization are fully benefiting from the relationship.

1. Am I addressing my mentee's developmental needs?
2. Do we both feel we accomplish something when we get together?
3. Are there expectations that are not being met—on either side?
4. What can I do to improve our conversations?
5. Am I spending too much or too little time with the mentee?
6. Are there some special issues that we should address (e.g., mistaken impressions about the relationship)?
7. Does the mentee see the same need for help now as he or she did earlier in the relationship?
8. If we have achieved our initial goals, what would be the next goals?
9. Am I still the person to help the mentee reach the next level of accomplishment?
10. Is there someone else within the organization who would be a more appropriate mentor at this stage for the mentee?

10

TEAM MENTORSHIP AND ITS CHALLENGES

Given the importance that teams are assuming in today's organizations, increasing their effectiveness is a critical business goal. And just as mentoring an individual can improve that person's performance, so, too, can mentoring a team. In this context, you would likely be called a "sponsor" or "team leader" rather than a mentor, although you would perform all the roles of a mentor—role model, advisor, broker, and advocate.

Cross-functional teams often fail because they don't have adequate management involvement, guidance, and support. You, as the team's sponsor or leader, can fill this void. Let's look at the various roles you will be playing.

- *Coach.* You will work with team members to increase their confidence and help them understand the full business context of project decisions. Where there is a team leader, your responsibility also will be to improve that person's leadership and problem-solving skills.
- *Catalyst.* You should stimulate the thinking and perspective of the group. Challenge assumptions. Play devil's advocate to help the team see more options/reactions and raise the level of critical thinking within the team.
- *Cheerleader.* You will keep the team motivated and work with members to address conflicts and other team issues that arise. Of especial importance will be your pep talks to remind the team of the importance of its mission.

- *Barrier buster.* You will help eliminate barriers that can include non-supportive managers of team members, resource problems, team member availability problems, or lack of tools, equipment, software, or facilities needed by the team.
- *Boundary manager.* Not only will you keep executives, managers, and others from meddling or interfering with the team's progress, but as you will learn in this chapter you will also span boundaries, acting as the team's liaison with other executives and managers.

Let's look at how to handle these roles.

TEAM FORMATION

In the first stage, the team is assembled and its mission is formalized. You will be playing a major role in this stage because you will need to decide if a team is necessary for this task. Teams are a very popular way to get things done today, but they aren't always the most efficient or most effective way to accomplish something. There may be another option for achieving the objective, particularly if you are mentoring an exceptional employee with both the skills to handle the project on her own and the desire to take on the assignment in order to advance her career.

A single mentee can accomplish the same goal as a team if the task is to gather information from others, for example. The information gathering can be handled by telephone, through e-mail, or by a one-on-one meeting in the office or over coffee and bagels at breakfast. The mentee, with your support, also can run a teleconference for a one-time exchange of information to solve a problem or to gather information needed to make a decision. Even the decision and implementation of that idea may not demand a group effort.

Remember, a good mentor is a good manager, which means that you create teams only when the individuals can bring together a variety of perspectives that will contribute to a better idea and when integration of different kinds of knowledge and skills can open networks of information not available to a single manager and increase acceptance and therefore successful implementation of the final idea.

TEAM STRUCTURE

Should you decide you need a team to accomplish your objective, your next step is to consider how best to organize that team. Do you want to bring together the best individuals from throughout the organization and assign someone to head up the team, or do you want to assemble a talented group but maintain the leadership role yourself?

Let's assume that you decide that you will need a cross-functional team. Further, you want to assume an active role with the team—maybe even leading the group yourself. The individuals you select for the team should have strong interpersonal skills, but that is of secondary consideration to knowledge in their functional area if the project has a strong technical bias. If the project's mission calls for a major change in organizational strategy or direction, you should also review your list of candidates to determine which of those individuals are unafraid of change—you don't want those with caretaker mentalities.

You may think you know already whom you want for your team, but to be sure that you have all the expertise you will need, you may want to use a skills inventory matrix to ensure that you identify all the competencies you require and those on staff with such abilities, skills, or knowledge.

A skills inventory matrix lists on the left side the talents or know-how you will need for the team and on the top the names of staff members who could bring these to the team effort. You should not give thought to deciding who the team members will be until you determine which competencies will be important to the team's success.

Consider both those within and outside your operation. To be sure that you choose the very best candidates, thumb through your company's list of staff members on the corporate intranet. You wouldn't want to overlook someone who could be a key player in the initiative.

When forming a group, managers first consider those who generally take center stage in everything in which they involve themselves, thereby overlooking those who: are equally knowledgeable, if not more so than their more boastful colleagues; have an equally impressive track record; and have more time than their more visible colleagues because their know-how is less recognized.

List your selection of team candidates on the top of the skills inventory matrix and put checks in those boxes to indicate the competencies these individuals would bring to the effort. If there is someone who can bring expertise in more than one area, indicate this in the appropriate boxes. Their broader know-how may give you some flexibility in forming your team as well as keep the size of the group down; ideally, teams should not contain more than seven members.

If you have a mentee, you might want to consider that person for the leadership spot; in fact, he or she may even ask to be point person if it's a high-visibility team. Don't let your mentoring relationship influence your decision, however. You may be mentoring someone who is an exceptional technician but who lacks strong people skills—indeed, that may be the reason why you are mentoring that person—and team leadership demands someone with both the functional knowledge and the people skills the team needs.

Once you have identified the members of your cross-functional team, your next step is to get them to become part of the project.

ASSEMBLING THE TEAM

To make your ideal team a reality, you will have to convince the individuals you have identified to give time to the project. Depending on their positions within the organization, you may also have to talk to their managers to get the approval for their participation in the team effort.

In team management jargon, your peers are the "enablers" (or, possibly, "disablers") because they can authorize or refuse to authorize the use of any resources critical to the team effort—and that includes the time of "doers," or team members, and "supporters," or those who can help the team with information to which it might not otherwise have access. As the team's mentor, you will have to convince all you have assembled to work on your project. Then throughout the life of the team project, you will have to sustain their interest and enthusiasm.

Obviously, it is easier to put together a team to work on an idea that comes from top management. Your peers won't want to seem as if they are obstructing a corporate initiative; even if participation could create workflow problems, managers are likely to say yes to a request for a staff member's help and may even serve on the team themselves. If it's your own project, however, you may have a sales job to do, given the little time today's managers and their staffs have to devote to outside projects and the birth rate of new teams.

As I write this, I can't help but point out how the same traits that are so critical to your position as mentor in a mentoring relationship are critical in your role as a team sponsor, mentor, or even team leader. For instance, as I have written elsewhere, it is critical for you to have a network both within and outside your organization. If your image is one of someone who sees peers and other professionals as those you can use, then it's unlikely you will be able to get help when the need arises. But if you have the trust of your peers and are known both within and outside your firm as someone who will help others out when the need arises, then the possibility of someone extending a hand to you and your team is much greater. Cooperation is usually returned in kind.

Don't wait until the need exists to build positive work relationships with others. Begin now. Besides preparing for a time when you might need to ask for help, good relationships between you and other professionals make a workday go more smoothly. Focus within your organization, and ask yourself these questions:

- Do I believe that my fellow managers will be cooperative? Do I act accordingly toward them?
- When I am asked to lend people or provide expertise or information, do I share?
- Do I find opportunities outside of staff meetings to foster communication with peers (have lunch, for instance)?
- Am I known as someone who doesn't play dirty politics to get resources or professionally undercut colleagues to win favor and advancement?
- Do I have a record of trustworthiness and reliability that makes me someone others will want to work with?
- Am I appreciative of the pressures other managers are under?
- Do I involve fellow executives and managers in decisions that affect them?

Answering yes to these questions suggests that you have already begun to build bridges to other divisions.

Go further. If you are currently a team mentor, make a list of departments whose cooperation you may need in the future. What is your current relationship with the manager in charge of each department on the list? Do you know at least one person in each critical area with whom you are on good terms? (If you aren't involved in a team at present, you might still want to do this exercise, but think in terms of your current operation's needs and which individuals could help or hinder your plans. It's probably worthwhile to identify potential enemies, too.)

Now do one more thing. Identify those functions within the organization in which you don't know someone or in which you aren't on good terms with the person you know. Over the next six months, establish a good relationship with at least one person (preferably the person in charge).

As a second objective, make a commitment to regularly meet with those individuals with whom you are on good terms already.

REVIEWING THE MISSION

As a mentor, once you have assembled the team, you have responsibility for attending its first meeting to communicate to the group the importance of the project to you and the rest of management and to clarify the mission of the group.

Although you or your chosen team leader may have discussed the mission with the group's members individually, you will want to review once again with the group as a whole its reason for being in existence, the limits of its authority, and the date by which its work must be completed. Think of the team as the boat. You are the captain of a boat and the team leader, if you have one, is the helmsperson. You all have to agree on the destination before setting a course. Your attendance at the group's meeting will lessen the need for course corrections, and should make them easier on your helmsperson should you be forced to call for course changes during the team process.

It may help the group if it starts with a team charter; that is, a written document that defines your expectations for the team. You alone could write this charter if the team was formed to pursue your own idea; however, if the team is involved in a companywide project, then you will want to work with key executives, managers, and others to draft the charter. That way it will communicate accurately not only the rationale for the team and the members' responsibilities but also the criteria the team will use to make effective decisions. For instance, there may be decisions that the team can make by itself, decisions that the team can make only with input from you, and decisions for which the team must request input from higher authority. There may also be negotiables that the team must know about in advance, like the time it has to come up with its recommendations or the amount of money that can be spent to implement a final decision.

STORMING PHASE

During the storming phase of a team—the second phase—conflicts arise as ideas are exchanged and action plans are considered and people develop proprietary feelings either about their suggestions or about the roles they think they should play in the team effort. As a mentor, you will be needed for two purposes: coaching or counseling the team leader and redirecting team effort.

Whether the team leader is your mentee or not, you may find yourself acting as his mentor, listening to the leader's woes, sharing your own experiences to assure him that such problems are common at this stage, and helping him identify approaches for addressing the interpersonal conflicts that have arisen within the team. If a leader finds himself beyond his depths, you may want to role model those facilitation techniques that will enable the leader to regain control of the group. Your role as team mentor or sponsor isn't to coach or to counsel the team—that's the role of the group's leader. On the other hand, if you also are serving as the group's leader, then you will be responsible for coaching, counseling, and facilitating discussion during meetings.

During meeting sessions, there is a danger that the team, including the leader, will steer off course. As mentor (think "captain"), you have to be there for course corrections.

Assuming that the team has its own leader, and you are only the sponsor, you won't be at meetings, so you need to agree with the leader on how you will monitor the group's progress. Certainly, hold brief meetings periodically with the team's leader. But a simpler way to stay abreast of team progress is to be on the routing list of those receiving the minutes of each meeting. You will then be prepared to raise issues with the leader during your scheduled meetings. Members will also know that you are familiar with team progress when they see you copied in on the minutes they receive. The fact that you know the nature and quality of their contributions will motivate them to support the team effort as well.

As the team's sponsor, you don't want to become so involved in the team's effort that you start doing the members' jobs or the leader's work. Are there any occasions when you should step in? If you see evidence that the project leader is uncomfortable in the role or you discover that the leader is too inexperienced to manage the project, then you should take a more hands-on role in working with the team. Another cause for greater involvement is the existence of a strong interdepartmental conflict. All that may be needed is that you co-chair a meeting or two or help the team develop its team mission and project plan. If the leader needs additional support, you might want to mentor that person personally. In time, the members and leader will be able to work mostly by themselves and you will pursue a more typical resource-on-call role.

NORMING PHASE

During the norming stage of team management, the group gets down to business. You want to monitor progress to be sure that the team meets its timetable. So, during this phase, you will continue to meet with the team's leader for progress reports and to review meeting minutes. You also have two other responsibilities during this stage. The first is to keep the group motivated (see Chapter 14). The second is to support the team's access to resources and information.

Your ability to provide resources for the team will influence the members' enthusiasm so be prepared to call in favors or do some brokering for critical supplies. Each member of the team has a responsibility. Yours, as sponsor and/or leader, is seeing that the team has access to the resources it needs to accomplish its objectives.

If there is a team leader, you and this individual will meet to discuss not only team progress—the task—but also group dynamics. You want to determine how well the members are working together. Did all team members attend the last meeting? If not, why? Of course, you want to know if the progress is on schedule, but you also want to determine if there is true consensus and support for the team's most recent decisions or recommendations. If the team leader reports some interaction or progress problems, you need to determine the reason behind these. What has caused the change? Is the team enforcing its ground rules? What can you do to help? You and the team leader should come up with an action plan to get the team back on course. It may be a matter of the leader or you, as sponsor, meeting with a more vocal team member or offering support for a more introverted participant or the team may need outside assistance to take the next big step toward completion of the project.

TEAM PROBLEMS

There are several problems that you can resolve to ensure the team meets its goals. Let's look at some of these.

For instance, say a team member begins to miss meetings. He stops attending sessions or comes one week and then isn't at the next session. This slows down team momentum. Decisions are made without his participation—and sometimes remade upon his attendance. As the team's sponsor (think "mentor"), you need to quickly jump on this problem when it first occurs. Why has this happened?

There are several likely causes: lack of agreement from the team member's manager about whether the member needs to participate, lack of the manager's buy-in of the group's mission, or even suppressed conflict between the missing team member and another member of the team or the group as a whole. It may be as simple as a procedural issue, such as the lack of any ground rule regarding regular attendance at team sessions, or that the team member is overworked and doesn't have time to attend every meeting. Maybe, the team member feels guilty that work is being dumped on his coworkers due to his participation in the project.

At the very least, to address this problem now and in the future, you may want to add a ground rule about attendance, such as advance notification is required if a member can't attend, so rescheduling a session can be considered. As sponsor and mentor of the group, you may want to ask the project leader to speak with the chronically absent team member. You also might want to talk to the team member and the member's manager to find out what may be behind the problem. If there are valid reasons why the team member can't attend, such as a change in day-to-day work or priorities of regular tasks, then you may want to try to work something out with the team member's supervisor. If the manager is uncooperative, you can either go over the person's head to senior management or replace the team member with a new person who has the same critical background.

Let's look at another situation you may encounter as a mentor. In this instance, you have put together a team and it is overly dependent on you for direction. Perhaps you have been a contributing factor by attending too many team meetings, or the problem may be attributable to a culture that makes staff dependent on those at the top rungs of the organization. Consequently, team members are uncomfortable acting as an empowered or self-directed team.

What can you do? You can encourage the team to discuss alternatives, the pros and cons of each, and then decide what to do without you. When it asks you a question, you should reflect this question back: "What should we do?" Reassure the team that its leader knows what he or she is doing. Finally, you may want to stop attending sessions. If you must find out what progress is being made at these sessions, limit your attendance to the last ten minutes or so. Focus on what was accomplished during the meeting.

Let's look at still another problem—one in which there is a team leader. The team you and the leader created is moving too quickly, not undertaking proper planning, not setting ground rules for its operation, and not clearly defining its mission. What should you do?

First, you need to find out the cause of the problem. Do the members feel pressured by their managers to spend minimal time in team meetings? Do they feel pressured by the team leader or you—yes, you—to complete the project quickly?

Finally, do the team members think that the project is a waste of time? If they don't see any worth in the mission behind the project, they won't devote the time necessary to see it through.

Ask the team leader what he or she thinks is causing the team to rush ahead. Check how long team meetings last and how often they are held. If meetings are less than two hours, ask the team members (via the leader) if they could hold longer or perhaps more frequent meetings. Consider revisiting the team to refresh members' memories about the importance of the mission. You may also want to bring in a facilitator or trainer to familiarize the team members with the proper approach to project management.

You may also encounter the very opposite problem—the team is moving along too slowly. The problem may be with the mission statement. Is it too ambiguous? Does the team not sense any urgency for completion of its project? Does the team feel uncomfortable acting in a self-directed mode? Is the leader not running the meetings well?

Here, you need to be clear about the timetable for completion of the project. The team may also need training. You may want to sequester the membership for three to five days with a team trainer to make the team more task-oriented and self-directed. If the mission is too broad or unclear, you may want to have the team revisit the mission. If it is too broad, split it into parts on which subteams will work. If clarity is called for, you may want to step up and lead the group in defining its mission or you may want the team's leader to do so when you are present to answer any questions that arise.

PERFORMING STAGE

The performing stage is the final phase of cross-functional team management. At this stage, the group produces its recommendations or implements its idea. If the team project was undertaken for you, you need to review the results, then choose to let the team implement its recommendations or not.

Among the questions to ask:

- Do we have enough information to make our projected recommendations?
- Are we short on supporting documentation? Are there other sources of information that we could have used? Should we do so before submitting our conclusions?
- How accurate are the data we are presenting?
- Is the process for change that we are proposing overly complex? Can we simplify our methodology?
- What could go wrong? If something went wrong, how costly would it be? How would a problem affect other operations within the organization?
- Have we considered the effect of both internal and external developments? For instance, could an economic downturn severely affect our plan? (Depending on the proposal, get the group to think in terms of

environmental issues, market shifts, changes in government regulations, and the like.)

- What contingency plans can we offer in the event of either the internal or external developments we have identified?
- Is there a cheaper way of achieving our recommendation?
- Must we go outside for the resources we need to implement our plan? Could we accomplish the same goals internally?

We've discussed a number of problems that you may encounter as you sponsor a team. Even at this stage of the project you may experience these. One of the most serious is that some members of the team are not fully behind the recommendations that are to be presented to senior management. Worse, as the team is presenting its findings the members begin to argue about their differences. What should you do now?

You need to go over the list of questions above to see what could be wrong. Likely some team members did not voice their concerns during the group meetings. Maybe some members had ideas that they didn't offer or that were not fully acknowledged by the team. The conflict always existed, but it was hidden and true consensus never occurred.

Admittedly, this is an awkward time to discover that members aren't behind the final recommendations you were prepared to present or were in the process of presenting to senior management. The worst scenario is if you have just made your presentation and disagreements among the team members arise. At this point, stop the presentation, apologize to the audience, and ask for a day or more to review the findings to be sure that the entire team is on the same page. Let's assume that you thought you were ready to present and suddenly discover you aren't. Take time to bring the group together, with its leader, and determine the obstacles to the solution.

You may want to do a pro-con analysis of the solution and then have team members vote on the best action. Explain that there can be only one idea that will win, but the winning idea should not be so awful that those who don't support it can't live with the final decision. That's what consensus-building is really about.

Once you have reached a conclusion all the members of the team can live with, you can prepare to make your presentation to senior management.

In the next chapter, we'll look at these and other issues you will need to address as you mentor your team.

Managing Conflict within the Team

The following steps are so helpful that you may want to have them posted in the room in which your team regularly meets, as a reminder of what to do when problems arise:

1. Acknowledge the existence of the conflict.
2. Put the problem or conflict in perspective to the overall goal of the project.
3. Look for common ground.
4. Let everyone air their viewpoints on any issues involving them.
5. Emphasize the common goal: to do a good job on the project.
6. Develop a plan of action that shows what each member will do to resolve the problem.

Team Ground Rules

If you have ever been involved in a team, you know that the members must set ground rules early. These ground rules are like a code of conduct for how the group will behave. Has the team you are mentoring set up ground rules that will be a solid backbone for the group's actions? Look at this list to determine how well your guidelines stand up.

- All team members are treated equally. Job titles mean nothing in a meeting.
- All views are important. Team members are encouraged to contribute fully to the group to realize synergy, achieve a thorough review of various options, and reach consensus.
- Meetings start and stop on time.
- Members commit to meetings. They make their own managers aware of scheduled meetings so that arrangements for backup can be made. If a conflict arises, the team is notified immediately so either the session can be rescheduled or the agenda revised to address issues in which the missing member is not critically involved.
- There are no side conversations while the meetings are in session. These are distracting, only add confusion, and send a message of disinterest of other members' remarks.
- All electronics—pagers, cell phones, etc.—are turned off during team meetings.

Mentoring Your Members

As team mentor, you should be looking for opportunities for the professional growth of your team members. Toward that, you may want to use the chart below. Under "Team Member," list each member. In the second column, identify at least one assignment you can give each member to help the member achieve his or her career goal.

Team Member   Growth Opportunity

Preparing Your Presentation

There are seven key questions you want to answer in your final presentation:

1. What was the project goal?
2. What made the achievement of that goal difficult and also important?
3. Who worked on the project?
4. What made each individual critical to the task? Be specific.
5. What were the accomplishments of the team? Pinpoint individual effort.
6. What problems were encountered that called for members to excel?
7. What aspects of this project make you as mentor (leader or sponsor) proud of your team?

Why Cross-Functional Teams?

There are benefits to be had from mentoring a cross-functional (CF) team, including:

- *Speed.* CF teams, when their members are appropriately empowered, get things done faster, particularly in the areas of product development and customer service.

(continued)

- *Complexity.* CF teams enable an organization to solve complex problems, bringing together people with different skill sets, experiences, and perceptions.
- *Creativity.* New product and service breakthroughs come from the clash of ideas, not from interactions among people with similar disciplines and consequently similar outlooks.
- *Customer focus.* CF teams focus all of an organization's efforts on satisfying a specific internal or external customer or group of customers.
- *Organizational learning.* Team members pick up technical and professional skills more easily, gain important knowledge about other areas of the organization, and learn how to work with people with different styles and cultural backgrounds.
- *Single point of contact.* The team promotes more effective and efficient teaming by identifying one place to go for information and decisions about a project or a customer.

C a s e   S t u d y

SATURN

The car company Saturn not only encourages informal mentoring throughout the organization but also supports African-American and Hispanic men's and women's groups that have come together informally for the purpose of mentoring.

On a more formal level are Operations Module Advisors (OMAs) who are in charge of developing the self-managed teams as well as their day-to-day production initiatives. In the first level of partnered leadership, OMAs come in pairs (one OMA is union, the other management) and are responsible for a module (10 teams) with a crew of 100 members. This setup lends itself naturally to mentoring. A new management OMA can be paired with an experienced union OMA on the job to make the transition easier and foster knowledge sharing. HRM at Saturn looks for good fits by using such tests as the Meyers-Briggs personality tests.

C a s e S t u d y

HANDS-ON LESSONS FOR
HIGH SCHOOL SCIENCE STUDENTS

For six years, Grace Construction Products of Cambridge, Massachusetts, has hosted a mentoring program for Somerville High School science students. Headed by Ara A. Jeknavorian, Ph.D., research manager at the firm's R&D laboratory, the program teams Somerville students with Grace R&D staff members to work together on a variety of science projects throughout the school year.

Grace is a leading global supplier of catalysts and silica products, specialty construction chemicals, building materials, and sealants and coatings. It has around 6,000 employees and operations in nearly 40 countries.

The mentoring program, begun in 1999, makes mentors available to students who want help with their science fair projects. "It's great to work with students and help them experience, firsthand, what pure science is all about. This program offers a golden opportunity for highly motivated young people to work closely with scientists in a world-class R&D environment—and our scientists also learn from the students. It's an incredible experience for everyone involved," says Jeknavorian.

Each year, Jeknavorian recruits mentors from Grace's R&D staff. Scientists volunteer to act as mentors to the students who come to Grace Laboratories to work on their projects. The mentors spend a couple of hours each week, from late October to the beginning of February, working with the young people on their projects. The students do all the work, but the mentors provide them with guidance in the form of information on research techniques, working through project steps, analyzing results, and most importantly presenting their work to the judges at the science fair.

Generally, as many as 20 students volunteer for the group. They are separated into 12 groups and paired with one to three staff members. Neal Berke, a research fellow, worked with two groups on projects directly related to two of Grace's major business lines—concrete and cement additives. After his first year as a mentor, Berke said, "By the end of the program, most students knew more about research methodologies, learned how to use sophisticated equipment and apply safety procedures, had a much better understanding of concrete, and figured out ways to improve the durability of concrete while helping improve the environment." On average, as many as two-thirds of the student participants have gone on to state competitions.

Chapter

11

WHAT MAKES A SUCCESSFUL FORMAL SYSTEM?

What makes a successful corporate program? There are several elements that are critical, but what is more important than the components of the program is a clearly defined purpose. When a program has a specific purpose, it often has top management support. That can make its success more likely.

The goals vary with the organization's strategic needs or issues of concern among its workforce. For example, at Fannie Mae, the company's corporate mentor program is designed to encourage the advancement of high-potential employees, particularly women and minorities. To date the program seems to be successful. Women make up 44 percent of the organization's management, up from 36 percent in 1992, and minorities make up 25 percent of that group, up from 15 percent in the same year.

Said Rosina Racioppi, chief operating officer of Women United, a Hillsboro, New Jersey, organization that provides development programs for women in *Fortune* 2000 companies, "Mentoring relationships can help get people who have been excluded into the pipeline."

Some organizations have more than one mentoring program, each with a different specific purpose. Once they have been successful with a mentoring program, they consider another way in which mentoring will help the organization.

But the key is that each program has a specific goal, whether it is to acquaint new hires with the company faster or to cross-train two departments, such as sales and marketing, R&D and manufacturing, or IT and sales. For commitment to the program, the company needs to have a clear understanding of what the mentoring program is intended to do and communicate that to employees.

IDENTIFYING YOUR FIRM'S INTEREST

Why are you and your organization considering undertaking a mentoring program? Below I've listed 15 major reasons why mentoring programs are used today. This is far from a complete list, but it will get you to start thinking. Which of these statements applies to your company?

1. You want to supplement or replace leadership training with a mentoring program.
2. You want to accelerate the development of top performers.
3. You want to increase representation of minority interests in management.
4. You want to help low and mediocre performers.
5. You want to revitalize midcareer executives.
6. You want to recruit top performers and keep the very best of your employees.
7. You want to shorten learning curves for new hires.
8. You want to close skill and ability gaps of existing staff members.
9. You want to help professionals obtain certification.
10. You want a solid management staff.
11. You want to ensure each senior executive has a successor waiting in the wings.
12. You want to support classroom or e-learning with real-life experience under the direction of an experienced executive.
13. You want to have a structure in place to support those who have a need for personal individual growth, including building self-esteem.
14. You want to prepare key personnel for the competencies that a major change in operations will demand.
15. You want to tie your clients to key personnel by having a staff person mentor the client rep in the use of your company's product or service.

Whatever the program's objectives, you want to set very clear, identifiable, and, most important, realistic goals for your program. You can only validate the worth of your mentoring initiative if you have quantifiable objectives, so consider how this might be possible. Many successful programs point to higher retention rates or better recruitment efforts. An increase in promotion of women or minority members, if that is an objective, can also be quantified. Skill improvements can be measured by performance assessments of protégés by their supervisors. Likewise, advancement among protégés into leadership positions compared to nonprotégés can also validate your program.

An increase in customer retention can be used to demonstrate the success of a mentoring program when the increase occurs as a result of pairing a staff member with a client rep.

As you initiate your program, you want to make it clear to those within your organization your purpose for the program. For instance, "Our mentoring effort is aimed at increasing employee retention from X percent to Y percent over a three-year period," or "This mentoring program should increase the number of managerial and executive jobs we can fill by internal recruitment from A percent to B percent over 18 months." Such clarity is important because it will help encourage applications for the role of mentor in the program, as well as for those who would want to serve as mentees.

Assuming that your expectations are realistic, this information is equally important to present to senior management to get their approval to initiate the mentoring effort. It won't be sufficient to go to senior management with a proposal that promises to develop people "to their fullest potential." While mentoring programs can do that very thing, you need to be able to demonstrate the impact on your organization's human capital to get investment in the program. There will be a cost to the program, but actual costs will depend on the amount of involvement and nature of the program. Often, companies begin with a pilot program to monitor results. Assuming that these are good, the organization will move forward with the program, often extending it beyond the initial planned boundaries.

Initial efforts also enable the organization's management to identify ways to improve the quality of the program and to reduce the administrative time and operating costs of the effort.

The intent of the program will influence the duration of mentor-mentee relationships. Other factors that influence the relationships are the development goals of the protégés, the frequency of contact, and the geographical proximity between mentors and mentees.

A MENTORING CULTURE

Almost as important as a clearly defined purpose is a culture that will support the mentoring effort. Ideally, you should have a learning organization that looks for opportunities to foster professional development in all its employees. From first-line management to the very top of the organization, senior management must acknowledge the need for people in the organization to be given the opportunity to utilize fully their talent. It isn't enough for the organization to talk about giving its employees an opportunity to advance, or even to commit to it in writing in its mission statement. You want everyone—from the CEO's office to the clerk in the mailroom—to walk that talk.

If you are a fan of *Star Trek: The Next Generation*, you may be familiar with the three-word phrase that Jean-Luc Picard uses to empower his top team: "Make it so." A learning culture enables senior management to reap the full benefits of a mentoring program with a single, "Make it so." As Lois J. Zachary writes in *The Mentor's Guide* (Jossey-Bass): "Organizations spend significant time and money developing mentoring programs. Some programs are successful for a limited period of time, while others continue to thrive and grow. The difference between the two lies in sustainability. Mentoring programs enjoy sustainability over time when mentoring is embedded in an organizational culture that values continuous learning."

We are not only talking, here, about skill training for outstanding on-the-job performance or even professional development training for mentees to prepare them for future career moves, but also training in mentoring itself. Both mentors and mentees need to be prepared for their new relationship. Certainly mentors and mentees can better understand their roles in structured programs by talking to friends and family members who have mentored or have been mentored by another. But some of the most progressive—and successful—programs bring in experts in communication and coaching, as well as mentoring itself, to prepare mentor and mentee candidates for the coupling to come in the future. Some organizations encourage existing informal mentoring pairs to participate in the training and education programs that are a part of the facilitated program.

GETTING THE PROGRAM OFF THE GROUND

Ideally, if there has been some informal mentoring taking place, and people speak well of it, you are more likely to get a positive reaction to the idea of a more structured program.

Most organizations deliberately start small—even begin with a pilot program. Two good targets are new hires and prospective leaders. If you are hesitant about either staff reception or availability of structure for a formal, facilitated program, you may want to begin with an enhanced informal mentoring program in which you offer printed materials to help those employees and managers who are already partners in mentorship relationships or are seeking mentors to maximize the benefits of their relationships. Monitor this informal effort for a time before proposing your idea for a more structured program.

In the interim, you might want to research other corporate mentoring programs (see the sidebars at the end of selected chapters for examples of several successful corporate programs), identify the goals to which you want to link your mentoring effort, and assemble a task force or team of managers and employees who are excited enough about the idea of mentoring to be willing to act as a steering committee for the program's startup.

THE NEED FOR TRAINING

Training can go a long way toward preparing participants and avoiding some of the traps associated with failure, such as unrealistic expectations of protégés and lack of commitment by mentors. Besides explaining the nuts and bolts of a formal program, the right training will let participants know that, as with any relationship, there may be hiccups along the way. Stumbling blocks like miscommunication, neediness, interfering responsibilities, and productivity peaks and valleys may create troublesome issues.

At the very least, the company should include an orientation program for mentors and mentees which provides:

- Program overview
- Description of eligibility, screening process, and suitability requirements
- Level of commitment expected (time, energy, and flexibility)
- Expectations and restrictions (accountability)
- Benefits and rewards participants can anticipate, if any
- Separate focus for potential mentors and mentees
- Summary of program policies, including written reports, interviews, and evaluation process

Training programs may be implemented by staff trainers or by experts in the field of mentoring. Besides training, these experts will play a key role in the development of the program. But such expertise can also come from in house. Often, structured programs stem from the expansion of informal programs or the initiative of someone in human resources, organizational development, or a member of management who sees the strategic value of mentoring.

Participants in formal programs believe that advance warning about the bad things that can happen can prepare them in the event that they occur.

Participants are willing to talk out the difficulty with the other party rather than hold in their feelings.

For instance, protégés may expect more than their mentors are giving, yet say nothing. Perhaps their mentors may want to focus on a number of issues, many of importance to the organization, whereas the protégés are interested in working solely on their careers.

Maybe neither mentor nor protégé knows who does what in the relationship. For instance, is it the mentor who picks up the phone to call the protégé or the protégé who calls first. Training can address these issues and make the early stages of the relationship go more smoothly.

Some companies extend training beyond the pair to the supervisor of the mentee. They offer an orientation program to relieve concerns that the protégé's manager may have about the special attention an employee may be receiving. Too often, there is lack of buy-in by managers and supervisors. They see mentoring as a threat, not as an opportunity to wind up with more skilled staff members.

Consequently, you need to approach supervisors by asking, "What specifically do you think a mentoring program could do for you?" instead of, "Do you think a mentoring program would be helpful to you as a manager?" Involve your management staff in agreeing to the objectives of the program, thereby starting the whole process of buy-in.

Those supporting the program should set aside an hour or so, maybe over lunch time, to make a presentation regarding the proposed mentoring program and seeking input on its objectives. Invite all the managers and supervisors likely to be affected, offering them the opportunity to contribute to the discussion. Those who don't attend will appreciate the offer being made, and will acknowledge that they were given a voice in the program, even if they didn't participate. If only a few managers attend, look at the bright side. The smaller numbers will make for a more manageable, focused meeting. Who knows, some attendees may turn into advocates of the program.

GIVING BACKBONE TO THE PROGRAM

Whoever champions the program needs to look beyond how the mentor and mentee pools will be created, the pairing protocols, the participants' roles and responsibilities, and the name of the program (it always amazes me the things people focus on), to set the background for the program. This includes identifying ways beyond the personal positive feelings that come from participation in a mentoring program to determine ways to reward, recognize, and celebrate mentoring success. For instance:

- Should excellence in mentoring be recognized?
- How should accomplishments be celebrated?
- Should all participants be recognized and rewarded?

While no organization should promise either the mentor or mentee a promotion from participation in the program, ideally the opportunity to promote those who have developed professionally from their participation should not be overlooked. Alternatively, a company might want to consider a "Mentor of the Year" award for an executive or manager who stood out from the other mentors in the program based on mentee assessments or other criteria set. Rather than give a bonus, a financial award may be given that the recipient may be able to donate to a favorite charity, as one corporate program allows.

Mentees enter these programs to advance in their careers and to gain additional learning experiences to build and demonstrate their capabilities. If they discover that success means nothing more than qualifying for more responsibility—no raise, no promotion—then a program can die from attrition as participants and future participants realize that the program is nothing more than a bromide to discourage talented people from seeking opportunities outside their current company. The career goals that are set should be realistic and mentees who have demonstrated new skills should be considered for new openings as they occur.

COMMUNICATIONS PROGRAM

Let's assume that you have received top management's approval to introduce a mentoring program into your organization. You will need to notify prospective participants about the program. Everyone in the organization—whether they are likely participants or not—needs to know what the program involves, how it will work, and why it is being implemented. Supervisors and managers whose staff will be mentored will need special attention. They need to understand their role and how it compares and complements the mentor's role.

Use your corporate newsletter to alert staff about the program. Post information and any components of the program on your corporate intranet. Depending on the size of the organization, you may want to take the program on the Web. On site, you can use posters, handouts, and brochures to encourage managers and employees to sign up as mentors and/or mentees. The communication can be both informative and motivational. Building a positive image of the mentoring process stimulates support and participation by mentors, protégés, bosses, and others.

CREATING A PROGRAM'S INFRASTRUCTURE

You will need to include in your description of the program how the program will be set up—that is, the infrastructure that will support the long-term viability of the program. Some organizations depend on a program champion whereas others turn to a coordinator assisted by a steering or coordinating committee made up of executives and managers who are willing to give time to help invest in the company's next generation of leaders.

In determining the structure of the program, you need to keep another goal in mind: You want a structure that provides opportunities for mentors as well as their mentees to share and review their progress. This means that someone or some part of the organization, like the Human Resources department, needs to be responsible for:

- Providing opportunities for mentors to share their experiences and their views about the effectiveness of the mentor program
- Providing opportunities for recipients of mentoring to share their views about the effectiveness of the mentoring program
- Addressing any problems or unmet needs that emerge during the program.

In some organizations, informal but regular social get-togethers over lunch best enhance the exchange of information that is necessary between the program coordinator(s) and participants in the program. Other organizations may choose to hold more formal quarterly or monthly meetings to accomplish this same purpose. The meeting structure may include brief reports that are written or given orally by mentors and mentees to summarize their personal progress and to identify any special problems or needs they have.

As a part of the planning, you will want to determine if the mentoring program will be a separate program or integrated into the firm's total development effort. If the program is coming out of the HR department, you should seriously consider integrating the effort into other career-planning, training, and development efforts. Even if it isn't within HR, you may want to work closely with the HR department. Independent programs are extremely vulnerable to economic downturns.

MATCHING MENTORS AND MENTEES

Earlier in the book, I described what makes a successful mentor and protégé. Let me point out that this is as important in a formal program as in an informal one. A mentor must be someone with a good track record at the company, someone who understands the politics of the organization, someone willing to make the commitment of time, and someone who truly wants to help others—not simply a manager who goes along with the program because it's the thing to do. A protégé must be open to feedback and willing to learn as well as eager to take advantage of the opportunity for advancement that mentoring offers.

Together, a mentor and mentee should make a good pair.

As I mentioned, a mismatch can destroy a mentoring relationship. The most successful programs are those that are based on best fit, such as experience, expertise, learning style, accessibility, and the like. Chemistry is an important factor, but it isn't the most important for the pair to gain the most from the relationship.

The methods used by companies to match mentors and mentees vary from allowing the mentees to self-select a mentor—in which case, guidance is provided as to how and where to find, select, and recruit an appropriate mentor—to highly sophisticated programs that are Web-based in which mentors go online (see the sidebar about Bell Canada in Chapter 13). In the latter case, mentors complete a profile that identifies their experience and expertise. Mentees search the site for suitable matches, ranked by fit, and then review the mentors' profiles. Based on that, they select the mentor they like the most and send an e-mail to that person. The mentor can accept or reject the mentee. Assuming the mentor accepts, it is up to the mentee to set up a meeting at which the pair discusses the subsequent activities. Likewise, evaluations are conducted online.

In between, you have mentoring programs in which the match is based on the coordinator and/or coordinating committee following detailed screening. Sometimes an in-depth questionnaire is used, and a committee of peers makes the final decision. Most programs also include protocols in the event that the pairing doesn't work out.

At Fannie Mae, each applicant is asked to complete an in-depth questionnaire that delves into their interests and expectations. Take a look at the questions below to see if you can adapt these to your program to ensure the best selection of participants.

- What steps have you taken to enhance your job performance, skills, abilities, and knowledge over the last year?
- What skills, experience, and knowledge would you hope for your mentor to possess? Alternatively, what skills, experiences, and knowledge are you prepared to provide your protégés?

- If you could have any executive or manager within the organization as your mentor, who would it be?
- Summarize your expectations from participation in the corporate program.

At Microsoft, all regular employees are eligible to participate in the career development mentoring program if they meet tenure requirements based upon their hire date. Mentors must have two years' experience with Microsoft, while mentees must have at least one year of corporate experience. A voluntary self-assessment tool was developed for mentors to determine their qualifications and readiness to participate as a mentor. The tool scores mentoring skills, experience, and attitudes and can be launched online with a sign-up process.

Data from Microsoft's main employee database are used to keep ineligible employees from accessing the Web site. Employees who do not meet the tenure requirements for matching can still access all portions of the Web site, except the matching tool component.

Mentors and mentees complete online profiles that capture job history and work experience data, educational level, mentoring goals and preferences (preferred focus areas such as people skills or work-life balance), and Microsoft competencies. Data points are processed through a matching algorithm that recommends the highest matching mentors from which mentees can then select. Mentees review the profiles of seven recommended mentors. Mentees who don't pick a mentor have the chance to choose again in several weeks. If mentors aren't chosen, they are thanked and notified of their status every 90 days. Automated e-mail notifications are integrated into the system to communicate to participants throughout the sign-up, matching, and selection process.

THE MATTER OF TRUST

Another fundamental element of a corporate program is the existence of trust between mentor and protégé. Both parties must believe that they can trust the other. While these programs may involve a coordinator or other executive or participant from human resources, and these individuals may be responsible for overseeing the relationship, both mentor and mentee must believe that there will be no breach of confidentiality about their relationship.

TIME FOR EVALUATION

After six months in the program, you will want to meet with the participants in the program to get feedback on their experience to date. If you have structured the program to monitor ongoing activities of the pairs, you should already have some insights into the program's success. Now is the time to get an indication of how the participants feel.

Evaluation accomplishes two things. Most obviously, it provides important information on how well the process is working and how close to the set goal it is getting. Certainly, this can help to get executives and managers who previously weren't behind the program finally to buy in. But the evaluation also yields information on how to continually improve the program.

What should you do if the evaluation shows improvement is needed? If the mentoring program isn't working as well as you expected, then changes are called for. But before doing so, get more data. Sit down and list your objective and subjective reactions to what has occurred up to now. What helped the mentees the most? What was constantly difficult and unproductive?

Interview mentors and mentees. Even talk to some of the naysayers who complained about the old program and were pessimistic about the revised program. Summarize your findings. Whittle down the ideas into a new program design.

Often, study of past programs suggests that more should be done with the mentees. They need truly to be ready to take a very active role in their development and the mentoring relationship. If you haven't trained them prior to the partnership, do so. Consider helping them negotiate partnership agreements (see Chapter 13) that clearly provide for their career needs. Help them choose specific skills on which to work and write their development plans. If the mentees complained that the mentors weren't helpful enough, teach them how to motivate and reinforce their potential mentors. Encourage them to organize events for themselves with their mentor rather than rely on their mentor to set lunch meetings.

As soon as you see a problem, reconsider the program. Go beyond "feel good" data to returns that demonstrate the worth of your mentoring effort.

In the next two chapters, we will look at two key elements of a formal mentoring program.

Would a Mentoring Program Work in Your Company?

Don't consider a mentoring program just because it is popular. Ask yourself these questions:

- What would be the business reasons for developing a program?
- What organization support exists or would need to be developed?
- What will be our criteria for success?
- Who is going to manage, coordinate, and oversee the program?
- What mentoring already exists?
- How will we pair mentors and mentees?
- Are there pairings we should avoid?
- What ongoing support, if any, should we provide pairings?
- How often should pairs meet?
- How will we communicate to our managers and employees the existence of such a program?

Assessment of Needs

An organization must be clear about:

- What is required from the mentoring program
- Which groups, such as women or minorities, will be specifically targeted, why they should be, and whether the selection will work against those who aren't selected for the program
- What level of interpersonal skills exists in management
- What resources are available to support a mentoring program
- How the existing corporate culture provides a supportive climate for the mentoring effort
- What exists within the organization to support or hinder a mentoring program (e.g., corporate policies, programs, practices)

O r g a n i z i n g   Y o u r   T h i n k i n g

Complete the worksheet below. Answer each of the questions and determine any actions you will need to take.

Question   Action to Take

1. What succession planning needs justify a facilitated or structured mentoring program?

2. How can I gain top management support for the program?

3. How would I organize the program?
   - Target group?
   - Department or division?
   - Levels?
   - Length of mentorship relationship?
   - Number of initial informal pairs?

4. How can I encourage manager and employee participation (e.g., rewards)?

5. How would I measure program success?

L e t ' s   M a k e   a   M a t c h

In making the best mentor-mentee matches, consider the attributes most important in the matching process. Consider surveying employees or holding focus groups to decide what potential participants consider the most important factors to be considered.

From a management perspective, you also want to consider how much effort will be involved in implementing your preferred process. How much data capture is needed? How will you store, manipulate, analyze, and report the data? What boundaries do you want to enforce around matching (e.g., geographical, job level, gender).

(continued)

Other questions you want to consider include:

- How will we handle unmatched mentors or mentees?
- How much input or oversight should the mentor, mentee, and coordinator have in determining match appropriateness?
- To what extent do we want to manage the process versus allowing the managers and employees to manage it themselves?
- Should willingness to take mentoring training be a factor in including candidates? What about time commitment?

SELECTION OF
A PROGRAM COORDINATOR
OR COORDINATING COMMITTEE—
AND THEIR RESPONSIBILITIES

While it would be wonderful to do without someone to monitor the mentoring effort, unfortunately someone is needed—especially during the pilot program. If a facilitated program is to be successful, experience suggests that you need a program administrator, often called a coordinator, to help bring together pairs of mentors and mentees, set goals for their mentoring relationship, and offer constructive feedback as they work together.

Corporations with structured programs say that competent direction is central to their program's success. Not only do you need someone in charge of the program but also a coordinating committee to advise, counsel, and even assist with some of the chores associated with making the program work.

THE COORDINATOR

The role of the coordinator varies according to the purpose of the program, but the program director or coordinator needs to:

- Sell the mentoring program not only to prospective mentors and mentees but to the supervisors of mentees and members of senior management who may be less enthusiastic about the initiative.

- Remove roadblocks to the program.
- Administer the program, which includes development of lists of pro-spective participants in the program; review of agreements signed by pairs, including the goals of relationships; and feedback on results.
- Implement the program communication strategy.
- Overcome difficulties mentors/mentees may encounter.
- Annually evaluate overall program results.

The time commitment is greatest during the startup, the planning stage, and the first two months of the program. Thereafter, the role of coordinator should take less time, so the position need not be full time. It is essential, however, that the coordinator's responsibilities are clearly defined, that the program coordinator has sufficient time early in the program to fulfill re-sponsibilities, and that someone is chosen for the role who has the pull to make the program happen. You shouldn't select someone for the role who may be unable to stay with the program due to changing work priorities.

PROGRAM CHAMPION

A frequent question of companies as they start up a program is whom to select to be coordinator. Certainly, it would be great if it was the mentoring champion—you—but you may have other responsibilities that would inter-vene with the commitment such a program demands.

Experience has shown that program champions may not necessarily be the best choice. If you are forced to change coordinators because of time constraints and skill deficiencies, you may have a program already at risk. Be sure that you give serious thought to the individual for the position. When considering time demands, it makes sense to double the time you estimate the coordinator will need—better to overestimate than underestimate.

Of course, besides availability for the position, you want someone who is truly supportive of the idea of mentoring. Because the coordinator will be chivvying others to participate in the program, he or she has to be a true be-liever in the program's benefits. But that person also needs the following:

- Familiarity with various mentoring schemes
- Skill at project management
- Position at the higher level of the organization—the coordinator doesn't have to be a member of the uppermost management, but should have sufficient clout and confidence to get things done

- A willingness to put in the time to make the program work—even if this might be in addition to current responsibilities
- Sufficient political savvy so that the planning and implementation can go ahead with minimal organizational conflicts

STEP BY STEP

Let's assume that you are putting together the proposal for a pilot program. Some of the tasks you need to consider include: initial preparation, marketing the program, planning the pilot, matching participants, and ongoing support.

Initial Preparation

Assuming that you will be working with a coordinating committee or team to support your effort, you want to determine whom you should select for the group. You certainly should think through your own role and responsibilities during planning. Indeed, this is the time to be considering your overall mentoring strategy.

Review the sidebars throughout this book to get some appreciation of the different mentoring models available. Most important, identify the organizational needs that the mentoring effort could address. Do you want the program to help new employees integrate more quickly into the organization or to develop future leaders by passing on critical skills, attitudes, and knowledge, or is your intention to give minorities and women more access to managerial positions? Once you have a clear idea of the direction the program will take, you need to identify the competencies—skills, abilities, and knowledge—that you believe your mentees should have to accomplish the program's purpose.

Marketing the Program

It is in this stage that you will be preparing a specific proposal for the program. This will entail awareness of those obstacles or roadblocks you might encounter and how to overcome or avoid them. In essence, your proposal will need to sell your vision of the program to others. One question to ask is the level of formality that you want your program to take. You can move slowly to a structured program by beginning with an enhanced informal program that includes training opportunities for both mentors and mentees. Whatever the kind of program, you need to list the tasks to be completed, the timeline for each task's completion, and the people who will be responsible for completion of these jobs. Include a budget for the program.

You might be better off first suggesting a pilot program. It should be easier to get necessary approvals for the planned effort if you begin by proposing a pilot effort. If successful, you can always suggest a permanent program.

Planning the Pilot

Assuming you get an OK from key decision makers, your next step is to confirm the participation of executives or managers who will help run the program. If you don't see yourself as the mentoring coordinator or director, you also will need to select and prepare the mentoring coordinator. You and those who will be involved in the first effort at formalizing a mentoring effort will need to determine report protocols—not just reports from mentors and mentees to the coordinating committee but also reports from the coordinator and his or her team about the program's progress. In addition, you will want to set up financial accounting/record keeping processes.

This is also the time to determine the mentor and mentee recruitment process, which means creating a site on your corporate intranet dedicated to the mentoring initiative. This will be part of the communication plan that will be used to engender interest in participation in the program. You also want to meet with the heads of various divisions or departments to describe the planned program, seek their advice, and, most important, gain their support. The more buy-in you get from those whose managers will be a part of the program, the more likely that it will be successful.

Be alert to what you hear from top and middle management. It's critical that you demonstrate a willingness to involve them in the program to gain their support.

At this stage, you will need to develop the objectives by which the pilot effort will be measured. What will be the pilot initiative evaluation procedures? At the end of a given time frame—say, one year—you want to be able to measure the value of the program using SMART—specific, measurable, activity-focused, realistic, and time-sensitive—objectives.

Matching Participants

It is at this stage that you need to begin the recruitment of both mentors and mentees and then create pairs. Once you have notified participants of their selection and partnering in the mentoring relationship, you may want to hold a get-acquainted program. Don't make it too elaborate. You want a low-key brunch or reception where the new pairs can mingle with other participants as well as spend some time getting to know each other better.

You may want to have members of the coordinating team available to meet and greet mentees and mentors and talk with participants, answer questions, and provide encouragement. Certainly, the program coordinator should be present to welcome the group.

At this point, you or the program coordinator may want to review with the pilot group the upcoming steps, including training for both mentors and mentees. Experience shows that such an effort is worth the expense and should be a part of the pilot effort. Some organizations combine mentor and mentee training whereas others have found the added effort of preparing mentees and mentors alone and then combining the two in a third and final training effort to be beneficial.

Ongoing Support

Once the program is under way, you need to stay in communication with the mentors and mentees, as well as the coordinator and coordinating committee. You need to make it clear to the coordinating group, if you aren't heading up the effort, to monitor the first few meetings to see how the give and take is working out. If it appears that a pair clearly can't succeed, it is wise to rematch the participants rather than force the mismatched pair to make a go of the process.

Executives and managers whose staff members are in the program need to be kept informed of progress and problems. Be assured that if they hear of problems, you will hear from them. Better to be open with them should difficulties arise.

In the first year—say, halfway through the program—you may want to offer additional training to continue to help the mentors and mentees improve their skills. You might want to hold the training session after asking the pairs and coordinating group to meet and review progress to date. Forms on which mentors and mentees can rate their partner may be worthwhile to get insights that participants are reluctant to voice. The participants should be asked to assess their partner on critical mentor or mentee skills. Has the mentor given the mentee the promised time? Does the mentor believe that the mentee is utilizing the opportunity to develop the knowledge that is being made available? Do both mentor and mentee consider the time well spent?

The Next Step

One month before the pilot program is over, you should ask the pairs to review their partnerships. Again, give out forms and allow the individuals to evaluate their partner anonymously. Once you have all the results, sit down with the coordinating group, including the coordinator, and analyze the overall success of the pilot and the success of individual pairs. What is your assessment of the program?

Like most innovations, you will discover some problems but generally, with some critical thinking, you should be able to address them. Sit down as a group and decide which aspects of the program to modify or eliminate. If you went with an enhanced informal program, you may discover—as many such programs discover—that a more structured program will work more effectively. Facilitated programs provide more direction to the pairs, including a written agreement between the parties that clarifies expectations and makes for a better mentoring relationship (see Chapter 13).

TRAINING MENTORS AND MENTEES

In Chapter 11, the importance of training was mentioned. Likewise, it was mentioned in the list above. Now let me go into a little more detail. There are certain key objectives of the training.

- *Unlearn past ideas about mentoring.* There are archaic notions associated with mentoring—see the Introduction—and participants need to understand the purpose behind the program at your organization. It is critical that prospective mentors and mentees enter the program with an understanding of how the program will support corporate needs and even its mission.
- *Make participants draw from past experiences.* If participants have had mentors in the past, they should be encouraged to think about the good and bad aspects of that experience and behave accordingly.
- *Redefine mentoring.* The notion that mentors are older, more knowledgeable, more senior personnel is outdated. The question of who is someone's appropriate mentor depends on the individual's knowledge needs. While some mentoring relationships today remain "top down," there are many instances in which younger, less senior people may mentor a senior individual who has less experience in a growing field of the industry critical to competitive advantage.

- *Mentoring is a partnership.* This means that the mentor should learn from the experience, not only from the mentee. In that respect, during meetings, the individuals may find themselves switching roles. Likewise, those who find themselves as mentors in this program may be mentees in another relationship, so participants enthusiastic about mentoring should learn more about both the mentor and mentee roles during training.
- *The limitations associated with mentoring.* Too many individuals become interested in mentoring programs because they see an implied process of promotion. Training should make clear that participation does not guarantee any special treatment, because such thinking could engender a lawsuit based on a charge of favoritism of participants in the program.
- *Participation is voluntary.* No participant in the program should feel compelled to be in it. Even formalized programs should allow participants to choose to involve themselves.

Corporate programs tend to rely on dramatic stories that demonstrate the impact of specific mentors on another's career and story telling, in which senior executives talk about someone they met in their career that significantly impacted their professional advancement. Demonstrations and role plays are used to help participants practice listening and feedback techniques (see Chapter 5, "Straight Talk") which can contribute to mentee empowerment and help solve problems. Because some mentors and mentees find it difficult to open up with each other, organizations have discovered that improvisation and other theatrical techniques can encourage more openness on both sides.

Throughout, I've been clear that not only mentors need training. In the past, mentee training was considered unnecessary—after all, it was assumed that their role was more passive. But increasingly, organizations provide a day or two of training for mentees to ensure that they become active partners in the relationship. Mentee training covers the individual's role and responsibilities, practice in listening skills as they apply to being mentored, techniques to develop a career development plan with the help of the mentor, development of a tentative mentoring agreement that incorporates elements the mentee considers important, the use of multiple mentors, advice in setting meeting agendas that offer learning opportunities, effective use of shadowing, and other aspects of role modeling, networking, and the like.

Mentor training teaches executives and managers not only how to develop their own coaching style but also how to better understand their mentee's needs and appreciate feelings, as well as words, expressed during meetings. If the mentor will participate in a cross-gender or cross-culture effort, there will be special training offered to overcome stereotypical thinking and other biases.

In some programs, participants will have chosen their own partners and know them reasonably well. In other instances, participants will not have even met. If this is the case, an orientation program is needed to provide activities that help the partners to quickly get to know each other. By the end of the training, the partners should have a basic understanding of the role they will play as well as an appreciation of their partner's background, current work, and future goals.

DO YOU ALSO NEED A STEERING COMMITTEE?

Larger organizations have discovered the worth of having a coordinating or steering committee to assist the mentoring program's coordinator in designing, implementing, and managing the program—from startup. The coordinating or steering committee can have as few as two people or as many as six for those programs with a large number of pairings. At startup in midsized and larger firms, a group of four is sufficient to monitor the efforts of the new pairs.

Why do you need a coordinating committee, in addition to a coordinator? Several viewpoints are better than one. A group under direction of the coordinator can think through carefully the overall objectives of the program, agree on the terms that will be used throughout the program, and finally nominate and vet mentor and mentee applications. The committee members can also decide on the best area of the organization to pilot test a program. When problems arise either in the direction of the program or between mentors and mentees that require third-party intervention, the coordinating group can support the coordinator.

Early on, as the program is first introduced, it can also help if you have several individuals from various parts of the organization involved. They can help sell the idea of the program to their constituency.

The committee will have real responsibilities so you want to select as members those who are respected within your organization. A coordinating committee isn't in existence to rubber stamp the decisions of the program director or coordinator. The ideal members are individuals whom you think would make good mentors (see Chapter 1) for not only managers or employees within the organization but of the program coordinator as well.

Consider the multiple activities that the team will be responsible for.

- Setting program goals
- Identifying mentors and mentees
- Matching mentors with mentees
- Conducting orientation programs
- Assisting in completion of negotiation agreements
- Tracking the health of the relationships
- Evaluating the result of the pilot test and conducting periodic assessments of the program

The right mix of individuals might be a program champion from senior management, a first- or second-line manager whose employees might wind up as mentees, and someone who shouldn't have any direct stake in either the program or any mentoring pairing. As the program goes on, you may want to introduce two other members to your group: a former mentor and a past mentee although not from the same pairing.

The coordinator could serve as head of the coordinating committee—a *sponsor,* to use a term from Chapter 10—and would turn to the committee for advice, or alternatively the board would have executive power and direct the coordinator. Of these two options, the latter may be less desirable because it might slow decision making.

Because you don't want to get locked into any bureaucratic traps, you may also only want to maintain a coordinating committee during the life of the pilot program. Once the full program is rolled out, the coordinating committee could be disbanded. Alternatively, you may want to retain the coordinating committee but only convene the group at the request of the mentoring coordinator to advise on specific issues. Finally, if you choose to have the coordinating committee play a major executive management role in your mentoring program, you will want it to continue indefinitely.

Depending on your perspective on the committee, you may choose to have the committee meet weekly early in the program development process and later monthly and even quarterly. In the accompanying sidebar, I have raised some questions that will help you decide if you need a coordinating committee. This issue isn't one to take lightly—in some organizations, its lack could create political or operational difficulties. So consider the questions carefully.

To fully appreciate the importance of the coordinating team, it may be worthwhile to review the group's responsibilities.

Facilitating Mentee Growth

Just as your mentors should be eager to contribute to the growth of talented individuals within the organization, so, too, should members of the steering or coordinating committee. They need to care about the development of others because most of their time as members of the committee they will be involved in helping others to develop professionally.

Members of the coordinating committee need to be good listeners who can judge a person's motivation level and needs. They also must be sensitive to the existence of problems that surface during the mentoring relationship. Often, mentors or mentees won't discuss these issues—they will be manifested in a mentor's or mentee's body language or in unreturned phone calls from one or both of the pair. The members of the coordinating team must be alert to such cues, analyze them, and then act quickly.

As such, they may serve as coach to either or both members of a mentoring partnership, from initial screening of the candidates to the conclusion of the relationship. For one, a member of the coordinating team may assist the mentor and mentee in preparing to negotiate their mentoring agreement or in determining career goals for the mentee. If serious problems develop in the relationship, a coordinating committee member may act as less of a coach and more of a counselor to work with a mentee who is frustrated with a career or a mentor who finds himself or herself physically attracted to the mentee.

Other soft skills that are critical are assertive communication, essential when an issue in the relationship has escalated to the point where the team member is sought to resolve it, and negotiation ability, essential for everything from the positive task of assisting in the creation of the mentoring agreement to the disappointing one of helping the pair terminate their relationship. Certainly, the coordinating team members should be skilled in providing constructive feedback to reinforce desired behavior and redirect problem behavior in the correct direction.

Analyzing Jobs, Tasks, and Needs

Coordinating committee members will be called upon to help the mentor and mentee assess the mentee's development needs—from skills to patterns of work behaviors to political skills. Knowledgeable about their own organization, they should be aware not only of the mentee's current abilities but also the tasks that that person's career goal will demand he or she master. Consequently, the coordinating committee member can help the mentor identify those learning experiences and training opportunities critical to achievement of the mentee's career objectives.

Promoting the Program

At least one member of the coordinating team must be skilled at writing and marketing, because an important responsibility is to design and develop exciting promotional materials to attract participants. The materials must entice but they also must present the process specifics accurately so that there are no misunderstandings on the part of those who do apply either as a mentor or as a mentee.

Matching Mentor and Mentee

I've discussed various techniques that are being used to match mentor and mentee. Let me just say here that even those organizations that depend on data banks to make selections need skilled coordinating team members who can review decisions made to match mentors and mentees and pass judgment on the pairs based on the mentees' needs and the ability of the mentors to act as resources for fulfilling those needs. Each member of the coordinating team should be responsible for monitoring at least one mentoring pair at the start of the relationship. Thereafter, the coordinating team member will be available to advise and counsel the mentor.

When the coordinating team member meets with the mentor initially, that person will describe briefly the background of the mentee selected and schedule any training for the mentor. Unless there is a serious objection to the pairing, the team member will then visit with the mentee for a briefing on the mentor's background and schedule his training.

Tracking the Relationship

Thereafter, the team member will monitor the relationship and see that it is healthy and productive. Depending on the nature of the program, the mentee may be asked to report all progress directly to the coordinating committee or work with the team member assigned to the pair. The communication need not be detailed—it may be as simple as a phone call or an e-mail every three months or monthly.

The mentee and mentor will share the career development goals and any action plans with the coordinating team and update this information periodically. Progress should be noted, along with any difficulties encountered.

Besides written reports or verbal assurances, the coordinating committee, under direction of the coordinator, may want to hold meetings of all or some of the mentors in active relationships, perhaps every other month, and also meetings of all or some of the mentees on the alternate month. The intent is to generate a dialogue in which mentors and mentees may express concerns about their relationship—which the appropriate team member will be expected to follow up—or to gain insights into how the program can be improved.

COMMON CONCERNS

As you undertake the program, you can expect a number of questions from both participants and observers from within the organization. Let's look at some of these.

- *What if the mentor actively sponsors the mentee so the mentee is promoted and I'm not?* You can avoid this question if you have communicated the role of the mentor clearly to your organization—sponsoring employees for promotion is not an aspect of a mentor's role. You can also reassure those not participating in the program by making sure that the mentor has little or no influence over a decision for promotion. This will entail careful matching of mentors and mentees so there is sufficient distance professionally that the mentor can't affect a mentee's promotion.
- *What if a mentoring relationship turns into a personal relationship?* Occurrences of this kind are rare. But you might want to implement guidelines, as a part of the program, stating that sexual relationships between mentors and mentees are prohibited, and that the onset of such a relationship will lead to the immediate termination of the mentoring association—and perhaps dismissal of the parties in the mentoring relationship.
- *What if the mentor infringes on my responsibility as a manager?* It should be made clear during training that the mentor is not to interfere with work tasks given to the employee by the superior; further, the mentor and mentee are not to discuss the line manager in negative terms. Emphasize that competing against the mentee's supervisor is not a mentor's role; instead, it is to complement the opinions of the supervisor

and to assist the mentee in developing a better relationship with the manager. Indeed, you should encourage collaboration between the mentor and mentee's supervisor early in the program to demystify what mentoring is for the supervisor and reassure the supervisor that his or her authority will not suffer.

- *If I receive mentoring, will my colleagues consider me incompetent or stupid?* This concern should be handled during the communication effort about the program. Should your program be designed to address diversity issues—the need to add minority and women to senior management positions—you may want to overcome any misconceptions by offering other employee groups the opportunity to participate in the program.

- *What should I do if our Human Resources department feels threatened by the program, fearing that it is assuming the department's role in employee and managerial development?* If the group is involved from the beginning, it is highly unlikely that it will feel this way. To avoid any concerns that might exist, you might make the department responsible for integrating the mentoring program within the training and development offerings. Thus, mentoring will be seen as a means to supplement or complement existing programs.

CONTRACTUAL COMMITMENTS

A critical part of the program is the agreement set between mentor and mentee. In the next chapter, we will look at how this document is best prepared and share sample documents.

Do You Need a Coordinating Committee?

- Does your organization have more than 250 employees?
- Do you have operations in more than two locations?
- Are there more than three operating divisions of at least 25 people each?
- How supportive is senior management of the program?
- Are there active opponents of the program within senior management?

(continued)

- Will implementation of the mentoring program be dependent on the outcome of the pilot effort?
- Are there individuals within the organization with past experience in the design and implementation of a mentoring program?
- Can you see disagreements on the senior level regarding the roles, rules, policies, or procedures of your program?
- Do you expect some supervisors or managers to be obstinate about the involvement of staff members in the program?
- Would you feel more comfortable personally if you had a committee to assist you in implementation of the program?

The more yes replies you have, the more seriously you should consider having a coordinating committee as part of your formal program.

20 Points to Include in Your Program Proposal

Whether you are program champion or coordinator, someone has to submit a proposal to senior management. Here's what that proposal should include.

1. The main purpose and subsidiary goals of the program
2. The direct and indirect benefits the program brings to your company
3. Why mentoring is better suited to addressing the objectives than other training and development schemes
4. The benefits for line managers, mentors, and mentees
5. How the organization can sustain a mentoring program
6. How the program would fit within the company
7. How you will recruit sufficient mentors, and whom they would be
8. How a positive response among the mentee target group would help the organization as a whole
9. The time frame for designing and implementing the mentoring program
10. How you would communicate the program to the employees within the company
11. Whom would make up your coordinating or steering committee
12. How the objectives of the program can be measured

13. What can go wrong with a mentoring program
14. What you can do to salvage a mentoring program with problems
15. What kind of mentoring model you would like to employ—one on one, team, reverse mentoring, or a combination
16. Whether the program would be formal or enhanced informal
17. Whether it would be best to start off with a pilot program
18. The scope of the pilot program (e.g., number of mentoring pairs)
19. When the scheme should begin
20. The budget for the pilot program

Am I Ready to Be a Mentor?

After mentoring training or just before accepting someone as a mentor, you may want to give the individual this 12-point form to complete to ensure that the individual is willing and ready to fulfill the role of mentor. Ask the prospective mentor to check all those statements with which he or she agrees.

1. I have a sincere interest in helping my mentee succeed. _____
2. There seems to be mutual interest and compatibility based on the information I know about the mentee. _____
3. Our assumptions about the process are the same. _____
4. I am clear about my role. _____
5. I believe I am the right person to help the mentee achieve his/her goals. _____
6. I can enthusiastically help this person. _____
7. I am willing to share my network of contacts, within and outside the organization. _____
8. I will commit adequate time to mentoring this person. _____
9. I have access to the kinds of opportunities that can support this person's learning. _____
10. I have the support that I need to be able to spend time in mentoring this individual in a meaningful way. _____
11. I am committed to the program because it will enable me to develop my own coaching skills. _____
12. I have a mentoring development plan in mind and will discuss it with the mentee. _____

W o u l d   Y o u   L i k e   t o   B e   a   M e n t e e ?

This form can be used by prospective mentees to identify their interest in the program. All interested employees would be asked to complete the form.

Name: Current position:
Work unit/location: Length of time in the position:
Telephone Extension: Supervisor's name:
E-mail address: Supervisor's contact information:

Please respond to these questions:

What do you consider to be your most significant achievements to date?

What do you hope to achieve by participating in the mentoring program?

What skills/knowledge/expertise can you offer your mentor?

What experiences would you like to have during the mentoring program?

Indicate any of the following skills, abilities, or knowledge you would like to develop during the mentoring effort:

___ Critical thinking   ___ Conflict management
___ Administration   ___ Team building
___ Personal productivity   ___ Strategic planning
___ Communication   ___ Project management
___ Political savvy   ___ Leadership
___ Business writing   Other _____

C a s e   S t u d y

UNITED DEFENSE'S PILOT PROGRAM

A mentoring program was the logical solution to help United Defense prepare and advance minority and female employees into leadership positions. The company studied other companies' experiences and found mentoring had a proven track record. "We were looking for a structured approach to achieve our objectives, and mentoring fit the need nicely," said Ted Kuriata who spearheaded the program.

The proposal for the program was submitted to senior management by a research team of five senior managers. The proposal pointed out how the program could address the development needs identified by its diversity council and employee surveys.

With senior management's approval, the group conducted a series of buy-in orientations—first to the general manager and director level and then to all managers and supervisors down to the first-line level. The objective of these orientations was to inform managers about the program—the why, how, when, and what. The armament systems division's pilot program was launched in January 2003 with 20 mentor-associate (mentee) pairs. These represented a good cross section of the organization.

The program is run by an implementation team of human resources staff and assigned coordinators from each major business group within the division. A "process champion" (Kuriata) oversees the program and provides the management impetus needed to remove any barriers that the implementation team may encounter.

Pairs are matched by the HR committee and coordinators, which review applications against an established standard. The recommendation is forwarded to the assigned director-level manager for final approval.

The organization promotes the program on its intranet site and in posters, corporate newsletter articles, personalized e-mail messages to the program's target audience of potential mentors and associates and then to the whole organization to solicit applications.

To ensure the pairs are successful, the firm held one-day seminars on the mentor-associate relationship for the pairs and a 90-minute orientation for the associates' first-line managers. According to Kuriata, these sessions were designed to inform people of what was expected from them and how the pilot

(continued)

program would be conducted. To help oversee the program, the firm turned to The Mentoring Group to provide fundamentals for structuring the program.

Still in its infancy, the program is being monitored carefully to see how it is working for the participants. Early results have been positive and there is consideration of expanding the program to include satellite manufacturing offices.

13

NEGOTIATING SOUND MENTORING AGREEMENTS AND EVALUATING RESULTS

Once a mentor and mentee are matched, it is important that they reach agreement about how they will work together. Most problems with mentoring partnerships stem from the lack of a clear understanding about how the mentor and mentee plan to accomplish the mentee's career development goals.

The success of a mentoring partnership is determined by the clarity and reasonableness of expectations of the parties in the new relationship. These expectations need not be written down. Research has shown that mentor and mentee pairs are successful with and without written agreements. In informal relationships, discussion of the rules by which the pair will work seems sufficient. However, as programs become more structured, and the need to evaluate the return from the time and effort invested grows, having a document that sets the guidelines for the pair's relationship and enables coordinators to monitor the relationship seems to have worth. (See the sample agreements in this chapter.)

NEGOTIATED AGREEMENTS

Let's assume that your firm's program includes a written agreement. Further, your firm has a coordinator and even a steering or coordinating committee. The written agreement completed by the mentor and mentee likely will need to be reviewed by the coordinator and steering committee and also by the mentee's supervisor.

The supervisor's input can be extremely valuable in helping to direct the development effort in areas where a need for positive change in the mentee's performance is seen.

We know that the mentee may expect to improve skills, gain political skills, and increase the chances of being promoted. The mentor will expect to be respected, admired, and, perhaps, to get an extra pair of hands to help carry out work tasks. These will likely be reflected in the agreement of the two, but the contents of the document must go further. The role of the mentor and the goals of the mentee need to be specified.

THE ROLE OF THE MENTOR

What can the protégé expect from his mentor? For instance, the mentor may plan to do no more than serve as a role model for the protégé, providing opportunities for the protégé to observe him at work. Time may be scheduled to discuss the protégé's observations and answer her questions after the fact. On the other hand, the mentor may agree to act as an observer of the protégé and work on some specific task tied to the career goals. Again, time would be scheduled for feedback and perhaps for coaching to improve performance in the future.

The mentor may even go further, offering to act as a guide in preparing the mentee for a specific responsibility or task. The mentor may agree to model the desired behaviors, demonstrate, or coach the protégé. The protégé can also be assigned projects that will give her hands-on experience with the task.

Why be so specific about the mentor's role? If it is established ahead of time, there should be no hurt feelings on the part of the mentee if she believes that the mentor isn't giving sufficient time to her career needs. Also, the mentor need not feel guilty that he isn't available each and every time the mentee needs help.

THE MENTEE'S GOALS

In Chapter 4, "Mentor as Career Counselor," you learned about how and why a career development plan is critical to focus the attention of mentee and mentor on some specific objectives. This plan should be brought by the protégé to his first meeting with the mentor. The mentee may write the plan on his own or with the assistance of his supervisor. At the very least, before the mentee shows the plan to the mentor, he may want to show it to his boss for feedback. On the other hand, some formal programs require that a mentee's manager review the plan before the mentor sees it and that it also be reviewed by the program's coordinator and the steering or coordinating committee before it is shown to the mentor.

This career plan becomes the foundation for the agreement between the mentee and mentor, which will specify how the development goal is to be achieved via mentoring activities.

The content of the agreement will depend on the nature of the mentee's plan. If the mentor and mentee agree to spend their time helping the mentee learn a few new skills to prepare him for promotion in the future, the agreement will be pretty easy to complete, listing the specific training activities that the mentor will provide to assist the mentee. On the other hand, if the mentee's career plan indicates a desire by him to increase political contacts or gain a greater awareness of cultural values, the agreement may be more complex, for accomplishment of the career plan may take more involvement by the mentor in providing opportunities for the mentee to meet members of management and conducting follow-up coaching meetings between the mentor and mentee to discuss the mentee's behavior at these introductions.

Let's look at a specific situation. Janet, a mentee, has told her mentor that her goal is to improve her image in the organization. She said, "I'm good at my job, but my relationship with colleagues isn't great. I want you to help me improve my communication skills and build an internal network of colleagues." Jack, her mentor, agreed to help her choose some public seminars to take, provide honest feedback on her behavior, and model a successful interaction with others. Janet believes that if she can improve her interpersonal communication skills and collegial relationships, she will be considered for a supervisory job. But by offering to help Janet be more at ease with her coworkers and others, Jack isn't making any promises—he isn't even guaranteeing that she will improve, let alone get the supervisory promotion that she wants.

All that Jack should say when he meets with Janet is that he will make every effort to help her become more politically savvy. This is what he will commit to do verbally and even in writing—nothing more. Jack may introduce Janet to others within the organization, role model political skills, and even coach her about her communication style. But verbally or in writing he should not guarantee that she will tap into or be welcomed into a network within the organization, or build better relations with colleagues in the organization. That is a reality of mentoring relationships that all those who take on the role of mentor need to accept. Sometimes, even with a mentee with tremendous potential, the goal may be beyond the individual's reach.

Which brings up an important point: A mentor needs to determine how realistic a mentee's goal is. To what extent will other factors beyond the mentee's capabilities play in her achievement of the goal? Luck may even be a factor. When a mentor and mentee sit down to prepare a document or even just talk about the mentee's career goal, the mentor should offer only that which is within his power to offer. If the mentor believes that the mentee needs more than skills, abilities, and knowledge—like contacts both within and outside the organization to achieve her goal—and the mentor isn't able to provide those contacts, then the mentor needs to be up front about it.

This also is true for activities beyond the mentor's ability to provide. Let's say that Janet wants to head up a task force. Jack has led project teams—indeed, he is leading one right now. But he is not in a position to promise her the chance to head up a task force. He needs to make that clear as they discuss the agreement between them. At best, he needs to say that he will be able to role model the skills of a team leader. He may recommend to others to give her a chance to head up a team, but he isn't in a position to sponsor a group and put her in the leader's chair.

LINKAGE BETWEEN GOALS AND ACTIVITIES

Most written agreements include a worksheet that mentor and mentee can use to link specific mentoring activities to the mentee's career goals. The first column lists the mentee's goals. The second column identifies what the mentee can do to achieve those goals. The third column lists the actions of the mentor.

Let's say that a mentee indicates in the first column that he wants greater participation at higher levels within the organization, the chance to have his ideas heard, and insights into how he can improve his leadership style. The mentor and mentee need to discuss this and agree on what the protégé can do to achieve those goals. This would be listed in the second column.

For instance, the mentee might indicate that, to achieve his goals, he should make a presentation to senior staff, head up a project team on an issue critical to the firm, learn how to organize his ideas for consideration by senior management, and be more open to constructive feedback. Based on that feedback, the mentee agrees to work to improve his shortcomings.

The mentor and mentee then discuss what the mentor needs to do to provide these opportunities for the mentee. Keep in mind that the mentor needs to be honest about what is within his capability to provide. For instance, the mentor believes that he can invite the protégé to attend executive meetings but he's unsure that he can find ways that the mentee will make presentations at these meetings. While he can't promise speaking opportunities, he can offer, however, to serve as a sounding board for the mentee's ideas. For those ideas that sound good, the mentor can also offer to help the protégé develop a format for submitting the idea for consideration by the top management team. Given the mentor's position within the organization, he often has to form committees for continuous improvements, so he can offer his protégé the opportunity to head up one of these teams, of which the mentor would serve as sponsor (see Chapter 10).

To work on any performance shortcomings of the mentee, the mentor may coach (see Chapter 5) and also let the mentee shadow him when he leads a project team to learn from observing the mentor.

The mentor can also sit down with the mentee and his supervisor and identify formal training opportunities, like public seminars or college courses that the mentee can take to grow professionally.

CONFIDENTIALITY

Both the mentee and mentor should trust each other. As a part of that trust, the mentor and mentee may promise to keep confidential information shared during the mentoring meetings. But that may not always be possible, and the parameters of that confidentiality might be better spelled out. I'm talking about those instances in which the mentor learns about a situation that runs contrary to corporate policy or is even a violation of the law.

What if a protégé confides to her mentor that she has seen one of her coworkers selling drugs to another employee? Corporate policy, not to mention the law, demands that the mentor report it. This was the quandary that faced Ben when Sarah told him that one of her peers was buying drugs from another staff member. Ben told me that he knew that he had to report it and he worried that it would destroy the trust between him and Sarah. Fortunately, Sarah appreciated the dilemma that he was facing, and she decided that it was best for her to report to the company what she had seen. Given the nature of the situation, it was correct that the incident be reported. But let's say that Ben had learned from Sarah something less damaging but also sensitive like one of her coworkers was regularly arriving late and leaving early. Given the promise of trust between Ben and Sarah, Ben would be obligated to keep this information secret.

Is there a way around such a problem? As a part of the agreement between the mentor and mentee, the pair may agree that the discussion should be limited to only that information pertinent to the mentee's development plan.

TIMETABLE

Most formal programs run on an annual basis, but mentor and mentee may want to agree on the approximate duration of their relationship. Setting a time limit has two benefits.

First, the pair may decide to set a time limit that is actually short of what might normally be expected because this would instill a sense of urgency in both mentor and protégé, encouraging a more rigorous effort on both persons' parts. The action plan would take on real meaning if the agreed-on activities were scheduled fairly tightly.

Second, establishing an ending date reinforces the temporary nature of the relationship, thereby preventing overdependency by the mentee on the mentor and a sense of possessiveness of the mentee by the mentor.

Should the mentor and mentee believe that further time is needed to achieve the development plan, assuming both are in agreement, the timeframe for the relationship can be renegotiated.

NO-FAULT TERMINATIONS

There will be occasions when the relationship is best ended before the scheduled date. In Chapter 2, "The Three Stages of Mentoring," I identified some questions you need to ask yourself to determine if the mentoring effort isn't working and if it would be better if you both parted. If you or your mentee has begun to ask the question, "Is it still worth it?" then it may help if you prepared a written agreement in which you have included a clause that allows you to end the mentorship without any bitterness.

The agreement should specify that either party has the option of discontinuing the relationship for any purpose, discussed or not. If necessary, either party may also consult with the program's coordinator or the steering team for advice on how to terminate the relationship gracefully without finding or acknowledging fault.

FREQUENCY AND TYPE OF MEETINGS

In Chapter 9, "Traps to Avoid," I mentioned that a major problem can arise when the mentee expects more frequent meetings than the mentor is willing to provide. Alternatively, the mentor has promised to meet X times with the mentee, yet fails to live up to the promise. Talking about this early in the relationship, and putting down on paper the decision about the frequency of meetings can minimize this problem.

Ideally, the frequency of meetings should be determined by the development goals of the mentee. For instance, if the mentee wants to chair a project team, it may be necessary for the mentor and protégé to meet only once or twice over a period of months, unless something goes wrong. On the other hand, if the goal is professional development involving training in new skills for which coaching, observation, and feedback on the part of the mentor are needed, then more frequent meetings may be necessary—as many as once or twice a month.

The mentor and mentee may meet face to face, talk on the phone, or communicate via e-mail. Any of these can be effective. Certainly, phone calls and e-mail take some of the complications out of meeting if the mentor and protégé are located apart from each other (see Chapter 6, "The E-Dimension"). The more sensitive the issue, the better it is to have a face-to-face meeting.

Of course, there will be times when a mentee wants to meet with the mentor and she is not available. If this occurs frequently, the mentee will become frustrated with the mentorship. Should such a situation occur, program coordinators may want to advise mentors to make it their mentees' responsibility to alert them to the fact that they are not living up to their commitment. "If I start neglecting you, let me know. It's your responsibility to help me keep this agreement." If a mentee is so upset about a mentor's failure to live up to her commitment, the mentee may approach the coordinating team and have one of its members monitor the relationship to determine if the pair is not meeting enough to satisfy the protégé's needs.

If this is the case, then the representative from the coordinating committee may want to speak to the mentor. If the mentor can't find time for the mentee, then it may be necessary for the pair to part and a new mentor who has the available time will be selected for the mentee.

PROMOTION PROMISES

Some managers and employees choose to become mentees on the assumption that participation in the program will guarantee a promotion upon completion of the effort. Given today's lean organizations, most organizations today don't make that commitment. However, to ensure that there is no misunderstanding, the agreement between mentor and mentee should clarify that there is no implied promise of advancement from participation in the program. This fact should be made clear in the promotional material about the program, but inclusion in the agreement will avoid any misunderstandings.

PAPERWORK

Some organizations have a standard form that covers all these elements. Others allow the participants in the program to prepare a memo that covers all these issues. Still others don't even require documentation, although for best results, some notes should be made about the expectations of both mentor and mentee in the relationship. Only then can the participants truly evaluate the program's success. Such documentation also enables the coordinating committee to assess how the mentorship is proceeding.

PUTTING IT IN WRITING

The term that is often used for these agreements is *negotiated agreement*, and it is important when you, as a mentor, sit down to prepare a written agreement that you keep the word *negotiated* in mind. It would be great if you and your mentee begin by being on the same page on each and every issue that needs to be addressed, but that may not always be the case. So speak up if you disagree with any remarks made by the mentee. Because you both likely will discuss the issues prior to putting the document in writing, you may want to make sure that notes are kept. If possible, you want to be the note taker because it will enable you to keep track of the issues, proposals, and tentative agreements, and to make it clear that you will make the final judgment when there is a difference of opinion.

You may also want to offer to prepare the final agreement. This ensures that what goes into the document clearly reflects your thinking. Besides, once something is in writing, it becomes more difficult for the other party to object to it. If you and the mentee agree to prepare the document together, you may suggest that the mentee complete his part of the document first. This will send a message to your mentee that you are concerned about him and his interests.

Don't be cavalier about this task. You want to capture not only the essence of the agreement in writing but the details as well. Too often, mentoring pairs complete these agreements without being specific about their roles or mentioning the frequency and type of meetings and mentoring activities that will be provided to help the mentee achieve goals. "After all, we know what we said we would do," they say.

Even before you sit down to complete the agreement, you want to discuss your future relationship. Open-ended questions are particularly useful to get a clear idea of what the mentee wants—or, better, expects—from the relationship. One of the simplest ways of finding this out is to ask of the mentee, "What do you want?" You might want to follow this question up by asking, "Why would you want me to mentor you?" This will give you insight into how much the mentee expects you to be capable of doing to help. If the mentee has unrealistic expectations, now is the time to clarify the mentoring activities that you can offer or are willing to offer.

Finally, if you find some gaps between what the mentee wants and what you are willing to offer, you might ask yourself and the mentee, "What other options are there?" If there are other ways in which you can support the mentee, this is the time to outline them. Be sure that the mentee considers these acceptable before you move on to commit to the mentoring relationship, putting down specifics in writing.

EVALUATING THE RESULTS

Why am I putting so much emphasis on a written document that defines relationships between mentor and mentee? This is the paperwork that the mentoring coordinator and steering committee or coordinating team (see Chapter 12) will utilize to measure the work between mentors and mentees.

Evaluation closes the loop with the negotiated agreement, assessing whether the career goals identified in the document have been met. Further, the coordinator and coordinating team will be checking to see if the program has had the intended impact on the organization. Comparing pair performance against the negotiated agreement will determine if the promised activities were conducted and, moving beyond that, spotlight specific problems and opportunities. In that respect, evaluations will help those in charge of the program make judgments about how to manage the program in the future.

Such evaluations should be conducted periodically. Certainly, careful monitoring is necessary during the pilot program, but even after the program is a part of the corporate culture, program results should be measured regularly. Besides the pros and cons of the program, evaluation will give positive reinforcement to the participants. Both mentors and mentees will see how much they have achieved and how many issues they have tackled working together. Interviews with mentors, mentees, supervisors of both, and coordinators and coordinating team members should be a part of the evaluation.

Regarding the mentor-mentee relationships, you might want to ask questions like: "What helped to get the relationships started in the right way?"

"What hindered effective relationships?" "What were the common characteristics of successful mentors?" "What can mentees do to get the most of the mentoring program?" "How can we use these insights in recruiting mentors and mentees and preparing mentors and mentees for their roles and responsibilities?"

From a corporate perspective, those behind the program will need to revisit the original proposal for the mentoring effort and pull out the objectives to see how well these have been met. Ideally, before the program begins you should set measurable criteria to judge whether or not the mentoring program does as planned. Then you can compare the situation before the program to the situation after. Did the program achieve its overall objectives? If not, why not? In addition to the overall objectives, do you expect the program to have had a positive impact on other factors, too (e.g., turnover, skills, motivation, preparation for promotion)? To what extent was the program well organized? Did the program coordinator do too much or too little? How often should the mentor and mentee report on their progress (if at all)?

In the final chapter of the book, we will examine some unique purposes of mentoring programs.

M entoring A greement

We have agreed on the following goals as the purpose of this mentoring relationship:

1.
2.
3.

We have discussed the protocols by which we will work together. In order for the relationship to be mutually beneficial, we agree to the following:

1. We will meet _____ (indicate frequency). We will get together, as follows:

If problems arise, we will meet as needed. Either party may initiate a meeting.

2. We have looked for multiple activities to enhance the mentee's development and have identified, and commit to, the following specific opportunities:

3. When we promise to maintain confidentiality, we expect of each other:

4. We have set ground rules for managing our meetings and the relationship as a whole. Our ground rules include

_____

5. We will offer regular feedback to each other and evaluate progress. We will do this by

_____

This relationship will continue until _____ at which time we will review our progress and make a decision about the next step.

_____
Mentor's Signature/Date

_____
Mentee's Signature/Date

M e n t o r i n g **A** g r e e m e n t 2

We are voluntarily entering into a mentoring relationship that we expect to benefit both of us and our organization. We expect this to be a rewarding experience, with most of our time spent in substantive development activities. To ensure a positive relationship, we agree to the following:

We define confidentiality as follows:

Duration of the relationship:

Frequency of meetings:

Length of meeting time:

Specific role of the mentor (check as appropriate):

____ We have discussed the mentoring experience as a development opportunity and its relationship to the policies and procedures of our organization.

____ The skills which will be the focus of the current relationship are noted on the individual development plan created by the mentee.

____ We agree to a no-fault conclusion of this relationship if, for any reason, it seems appropriate.

_____
Mentor/Date

_____
Mentee/Date

Questions to Consider when Negotiating a Mentoring Relationship

New mentors and mentees can benefit from considering the following list of questions when they first meet:

- What is the role the mentor is expected to take?
- How will we deal with the issue of confidentiality?
- Who is involved in discussing and negotiating any agreement? Should we include the mentee's boss or members of the coordinating committee?
- What duration of the relationship is suggested, if any?
- How can the agreement be concluded, if necessary at a time other than the specified time?

Case Study

BELL CANADA'S SELF-SERVICE MENTOR MATCHING SYSTEM

Bell Canada was looking for a mentoring system that was self-administrative, inexpensive to maintain, and easy for all employees to use. According to Dr. Nancy Nazer, of BCE Associates, it found it in a Web-based system that offers online matching of mentors and mentees.

According to Nazer, employees who are interested in being mentors fill out an online profile that captures key background information. Prospective mentees, then, go into the mentor match portal and search for a mentor based on their interests. For example, if they are looking for a career in marketing, they would ask for someone with that background.

The employee receives a list of available mentors, ranked based on the employee's preferences. The employee can then click on each of the names to view the mentor's profile. Once the employee has selected a mentor, the system sends a note asking the mentor to look at the mentee's profile and either decline or accept the request.

The way the system is set up, HR doesn't have to be involved at all, thereby reducing time and costs. The site requires only one support person who spends two hours per month on support questions.

If the mentor accepts, it is up to the mentee to initiate the partnership. At the first meeting, there is an online agreement they have to sign. It's a one-year contract specifying the expectations and objectives for both the mentor and the mentee. At the end of the year, the system will send them an online evaluation as well as the opportunity to nominate the mentor or mentee for an award.

The award is an amount of money the winner can give to a charity of choice.

As soon as a mentor has signed up with their desired number of protégés, they are automatically removed from the list of possible mentors.

The program is still young but reports about the system are extremely positive. Upon startup, initial response was extremely rewarding—3,000 people went online.

14

SPECIAL SITUATIONS

This book is designed to show you how to help support your organization's efforts to build the next generation of leaders by assuming the very important role of mentor to one or more high-potential managers and staff members or a group within your organization with an important goal. But many corporate programs have a special purpose beyond that. In this chapter, I'd like to familiarize you with some of the new applications of mentoring. Often, these start as informal relationships in which management finds value. It then formalizes them into programs. Sometimes, the mentoring effort extends past the boundaries of the organization. Indeed, as one of my colleagues said, the application of mentoring is limited only by the needs and desires of today's organization to leverage the talent within the organization and maximize relationships both within and outside their organizations. Programs designed to break through the glass ceiling and offer opportunities for advancement to women and members of minorities in companies in which mentoring was traditionally for white males only represent one, albeit a major, development.

Companies are supporting mentoring programs that offer leadership opportunities for their tech personnel, focus corporate initiatives on reengineering and continuous operational improvement, ensure the transfer of ever-new technical know-how throughout the organization, and shorten the learning curves for entry-level personnel. In addition, they are using formal mentoring programs to create the next generation of leaders and retain corporate intellectual capital that might be lost as the current generation of leaders age and retire.

Let's examine some of these special programs.

BUILDING STRONG TIES

Some organizations have found that it is worthwhile to have their managers mentor contacts at customer firms, building relationships that contribute to increased customer retention as well as ensure the financial stability of these firms. In the public sector, some federal agencies have encouraged contractors to mentor subcontractors and suppliers to ensure these organizations operate efficiently and effectively. This is only new in that it is increasingly becoming an offering to customers. For decades, manufacturers provided training for customers to ensure effective handling, maintenance, and repair of their products. But as the business of business becomes increasingly complex, organizations have recognized that training programs may no longer be enough.

Today's ever-changing work environment raises new challenges regularly in users' work, and a relationship with someone from the vendor can help the user explore his or her options—many of which may not be clear until after the user has had considerable experience with the equipment or product line. Certainly, this is true with today's new technology and software programs.

WITHIN THE COMMUNITY

In the introduction of this book, I mentioned public programs in which corporate executives and managers give up personal time to help disadvantaged or troubled youths. There are numerous corporate and community programs. On a grand scale in Florida is Governor Jeb Bush's Mentoring Initiative that involves over 200 corporations and almost 200,000 youngsters.

In academic environments, older students work with younger ones to acclimate the latter to college life to ensure that they do well in school. Sometimes students are mentored by those already employed, with the objective of encouraging the young person to work for the mentor's organization upon graduation. Recent graduates are mentored by those in the same field with job experience to speed the new hires' assimilation into the organization.

Mentoring is the sole purpose of SCORE, the Senior Corps of Retired Executives, a network organization that carefully matches retired executive volunteers with entrepreneurs and small business owners for the purpose of these retirees sharing their business expertise with business novices and smaller business leaders. When entrepreneurs visit SCORE's Web site, they are invited to identify their question or problem and search for a counselor by expertise or by region. A nonprofit organization, SCORE, now over 40 years old, provides free face-to-face or e-mail counseling (think "mentoring"). Based on their own experience, SCORE counselors are well aware how another, more experienced individual's perspective on a problem can enable a businessperson to overcome an obstacle.

We're all familiar with outplacement programs companies offer downsized managers and employees. After watching how the unemployed provide encouragement to one another, some such firms have encouraged those who have gone through the process and found new employment to form support groups and share their newly developed skills and knowledge to help the recently unemployed to find reemployment opportunities. The Five O'Clock Club, headed by Kate Wendleton, serves this function on a formal basis. Yes, the organization provides formal coaching by experienced career counselors, but job hunters and those looking for career changes also hold group meetings to help their peers reexamine their aspirations, goals, and approach to the search for a new job.

WITHIN ORGANIZATIONS

In today's business organizations, we see mentoring undergoing several changes. For one, we see alternatives to one-on-one mentoring relationships. Such new models include mentoring in peer groups and mentoring within unit teams, which resemble the mentoring from support groups outside organizations and in the community, reverse mentoring in which those at lower levels within an organization mentor executives and managers as high as the C level (such as chief operating officers and chief executives), triads in which three mentors work with one mentee, and mentoring circles in which a single executive mentors several protégés at one time.

Reverse mentoring is interesting because often the mentor will mentor someone in a higher position—sometimes, even, the company's CEO. How do you mentor someone in a higher position? When I've asked those who are doing just this about their mentoring relationship, I have expected each and every one of these mentors to reply, "Very carefully," but actually feedback about the experience is very positive.

While the most frequent situation is a whiz-bang computer nerd or administrative assistant mentoring a computer-illiterate senior executive on how to use the computer, reverse mentoring isn't limited to such situations. Newcomers who bring industry specific information to their new employer may be asked to act as advisor to a senior executive asked to identify marketing opportunities in the new hire's former industry. One talented junior manager had built a Rolodex from strong networking skills that was the envy of the firm's field sales reps. He made a great mentor to the VP of sales, providing insights into prospective accounts and, more important, into those at these firms with decision-making potential. One general manager, known for an abrupt manner and tactlessness, sought out one of her own employees, well regarded by her peers, to help her soften her style.

If there is any problem in such relationships, the main one seems to be resentment by other members of the staff who see the mentor as being in an excellent position to reap the career benefits of their close relationship with someone in a higher level within the organization. Where jealousy exists, it can make it awkward for the mentor's relationship with her own peer group. In the case of the general manager who sought help from a supervisor with strong people skills, it was necessary for her to ease the resentment by clarifying the reason behind the supervisor's frequent visits in her office. "Annette was uneasy about the request because she thought her colleagues would think she would use the opportunity to curry my favor." At a staff meeting, the general manager told the department's staff that she had had to ask Annette several times before she agreed. "It also gave me the chance to explain that I was aware of a communication shortcoming and I was trying to do something about it."

The staff was pleased to hear that their manager was trying to do something about her lack of interpersonal diplomacy. The boss's statement also proved to them that Annette had not set up the situation to brownnose the boss.

PAIRS AND TEAMS

Just as in the public sector, peer and team mentoring groups are not always led by a formal mentor. The group members themselves provide mentoring to each other. They may form temporary pairs or subgroups to address a particular organizational or departmental issue, then disband and reform around a different issue. Experience has shown that these forms of mentoring work best for cross-training, team building, and bringing new employees up to speed quickly, like having several buddies on staff at one time. As individuals within the organization develop rapport, improved job performance would be another outcome of such efforts. As employees train one another, companies save money that they would have spent on formal training costs.

At AT&T's Consumer Products Lab, valued employees who should have been mentored were unable to identify potential mentors and consequently quit as they realized that downsizing within the organization left little opportunity for professional advancement. So group mentoring was used to match mentors with leading-edge expertise with small groups of high potentials who saw the advantage of acquiring intellectual capital from the mentors and the opportunity to participate in consumer product development projects on which mentors were working.

As I write this, I am reminded of a friend, Charlie, who told me about his first few months with a software firm. One of the most competitive firms in the industry, it put great demands on its employees, and Charlie told me how glad he was that his new coworkers were encouraged by senior management to support newcomers as they oriented themselves to the way the organization ran. "Steve and Jerry seem to find the time to spend with me," he told me, talking about his new colleagues. "There's so much to learn and it seems there is so little time to process it all. It helps me to know that I can turn to not only Steve and Jerry but Mary, Becky, Rachel, Lloyd, and Mikey," he said, "to help me with my new job."

They didn't have formal meetings, but Charlie's new colleagues were always watchful for when he seemed to need some help. They created a learning environment, sharing their knowledge, experience, and insight with the newcomer. Ted, who headed up the department, had several mentees, thereby forming a mentoring circle. As such, he was able to provide technical and organizational advice and guidance. He assisted the members of his circle in using their own knowledge and experience to help one another. Thus, the circle increased individual performance to the third power.

Because the organization's culture supports mentoring, Charlie himself became one of two mentors of a new employee about two years after joining the organization. Now a seasoned employee, he was able to provide the newcomer with know-how on how to work with the hands-on department head (think "micromanager," from what Charlie told me) while the other mentor, with more years in the industry, could bring to the trio his broader knowledge of the industry.

While these mentoring relationships are very different in organizations, they are similar in terms of mentoring relationships in general. The initial meeting, as with one-on-one sessions, has the group of three, five, or however many are involved, clarify expectations. As a group, the individuals determine the subjects to be covered and set the ground rules for working together. Of importance, of course, is determining the desired outcomes of the participants. Likewise, potential concerns, such as confidentiality of information and trust among participants, need to be addressed.

Meetings need to be held as set, and participants must honor assignments and attend sessions at the designated dates and times. After sessions, the group should be able to identify specific outcomes as well as make assignments for the next meeting.

While the group meetings may have a beginning, they may not have an end, in that the worth of the group interaction may be such that participants may want the relationships to be unending. However, there should be some formal evaluation, perhaps an annual assessment, to be sure that the goals and objectives set during the first meetings were met, and to determine what worked especially well and what improvements can be made during the next year. As with performance appraisal systems built around key result areas (KRAs), the group might set its own KRAs for the next year.

Sometimes, these alternatives to one-on-one mentoring just happen. But, increasingly, organizations are behind these programs. Sometimes, they spearhead the programs; other times, they look kindly on them, watchful to see if the experiment works before they expand either the number of participants or the program's reach beyond one division or geographic area.

Should such alternatives interest you, you must have a clear idea as to the purpose of the group and how to make it work. See the sidebar on "Making a Group Mentoring Relationship Work," at the end of this chapter, to determine if such a program is right for your organization.

MENTORING RELATIONSHIPS

Because mentoring by supervisors is a growing trend, it needs mention here, although you can review Chapter 8 for further information. This represents another development as organizations look for ways to keep top talent. Mentoring has been found to increase staff performance and also reduce turnover. At Varian Associates Radiation Division, turnover dropped 50 percent. While it can raise the same kind of employee resentment as reverse mentoring, it has some clear management benefits, which is why organizations support this extra attention to top performance.

Supervisory mentoring has been found to:

- *Shorten learning curves.* Taking a new and talented staff member under your wing, even for a short time, puts that person on a high-performance fast track.

- *Increase communication of corporate values.* Not only will managers be able to communicate the company's values—values having to do with quality of customer service, the kinds of relationships expected among coworkers, the sense of teamwork expected of everyone, and shared responsibility for corporate profitability—but they will be able to explain the strategic importance of the values. If a supervisor shares with a talented newcomer how important these values are to the company's success, and in some instances, to its very survival, the talented new recruit, with a fresh perspective, may come up with an idea or some unique way to achieve the corporate mission or its strategic goals.
- *Reduce turnover.* This may seem unimportant in bad economic times when news of downsized companies appears daily, but the key point here is retaining high-potential employees and those in hard-to-fill positions. Once you find one of those employees who has agreed to work for you, you want that person to stay. If you can't offer big bucks or a promotion, you can promise that you will set career goals and mentor him or her to achieve them. Having an advisor and friend in a higher position in a company can be more valuable than the financial compensation of a bonus after one, two, or three years with a company.
- *Increase employee productivity.* The extra instruction that mentees get can motivate them to work harder, to take on challenging assignments, and to operate outside their boxes with some direction from their mentor. Thus the potential of these talented workers is tapped.

Mentoring is particularly helpful in maintaining the top performance of your superstars, individuals who can easily become frustrated when they realize that their hard work isn't going to get them a quick promotion or big bonus.

What about the benefits to the supervisor mentor? The mentee can take on projects that are important to the supervisor's department or division but for which the supervisor wouldn't otherwise have the time. The mentor manager can pursue ideas that could increase the operation's bottom line while being assured that many of the more traditional projects are being handled. Over time, as mentees advance in their careers and gain influence within the organization, they can also be the friends that these mentors turn to for key resources or support for their own ideas.

Assuming that those who get this added attention are seen by their peers as worthy of the extra opportunities, mentoring subordinates can stimulate performance throughout the department or division, as other employees work to earn the same special attention.

So the reason for management's support of supervisors as mentors should be evident.

CROSS-GENDER MENTORING

Cross-gender mentoring is exactly what it sounds like. Either males or females mentor protégés of the other sex to overcome sexual stereotypes. Many organizations have been prompted to do this by the desire to leaven the workplace and achieve sexual balance and fairness in senior management positions. Often, such programs begin informally and then are taken under the organization's wing. A case in point is the mentoring initiative for women in Asia begun by World Bank in 1997. Since then, the organization has begun over 16 programs. Each program has its own coordinator, and these coordinators—all of whom have full-time jobs—meet every two months to discuss progress. Coordinators are expected to have good interpersonal skills and not only a commitment to the mentoring effort but also to the bank itself—they must agree to stay with the bank for the next five years. Mentors are allowed two mentees.

Each mentoring group has its own steering committee of six to eight employees who plan social gatherings, match mentors to employees, and otherwise oversee program activities. Training is provided for both mentors and mentees. In pairing mentors and mentees, the mentoring committees check to see that no reporting relationship exists and that there is at least one grade level that separates mentors from mentees. An effort is made to match cultural similarities and educational levels, like pairing a Ph.D. with an employee with a doctorate.

After two months in the program, mentoring partners are asked if they are meeting and how the mentoring process is working. Mentees are not asked if they like or dislike their mentors. Instead, there is oral feedback and also a written evaluation that allows each partner to rate the pair's progress in career planning, discussion of organizational culture, and development of interpersonal skills. A third evaluation is used to get feedback from the pair on the mentorship level achieved. The World Bank has also used an outside firm to do a final evaluation to measure the return on the partnership.

At Aer Rianta in Dublin, which manages three international airports at Dublin, Cork, and Shannon, in the Republic of Ireland, a Women in Management program came about in 1992. At the time, a study of women's representation throughout the organization found that there had been an influx of women into management in the previous two years but it still only represented 14 percent of the total management positions in the company and most of these were at the lower management levels. This was true despite the fact that considerable numbers of women were entering the company. They were filling lower management positions, but senior management continued to be an exclusively male preserve.

A meeting of the women managers with the company's CEO and manager of equal opportunities development identified several of the barriers to women's progression and participation at management levels. One of the solutions to emerge was an "understudy" program where women managers would be paired with more senior male colleagues to learn by observation and discussion. As discussion continued, the program was renamed mentoring to reflect its true purpose.

Launched in 1993, it involved 18 women managers being mentored by an equal number of male senior managers in the company. The manager of equal opportunities and a senior colleague attempted to match mentors and mentees as closely as possible to each mentee's individual needs, taking into account her declared preferences and also developmental opportunities. All mentors and mentees were volunteers.

The experience was more difficult for the mentees than the mentors, as can be expected, but the first year was sufficiently positive for the organization to decide to continue the scheme. However, both mentors and mentees agreed that they needed to set clear objectives to work toward. As one mentee said, "We had no agenda and no objectives. We managed the relationship by discussing each other's work and different management styles." On a more positive note, a mentee remarked, "One of the benefits of mentoring is how it forces you to stop and think about your own managing techniques."

If there was one major change in the program, it was a better understanding about the need to invest time not just in the meetings but in preparation and follow-up questioning.

What have been the results to date? As of 2000, four mentees have been promoted and many of the others are seen to have increased their potential sufficiently to be candidates for promotion in the next few years. One now works directly for her former mentor and the mentoring relationship continues. But the biggest measure of success is that male managers at the same level as the women mentees have asked to be included.

This appears to be a pattern. At Exxon's sales division, a structured mentoring program was instituted when it was found that informal mentoring was performed by white male managers for other white males. This led to a disproportionate staff turnover among women and minorities, who felt they had less growth opportunity than their white male counterparts. Indeed, white males who had been mentored experienced improved performance and qualified for and earned promotions. Once women and minorities had the opportunity to benefit from mentoring, they reported feeling more valued. The existence of a formal program prompted the males in the organization to request admittance into the program as well.

WORKFORCE DIVERSITY

Similar in purpose to the gender-focused mentoring programs are those programs designed to create a level playing field for members of racial and ethnic minorities. By enabling diverse groups to participate and contribute more equally to the advancement of the organization, more people benefit. Indeed, mentoring across differences—racial, ethnic, cultural, you name it—can be an exciting experience for mentor and protégé alike. No other relationship, done correctly, poses such promise for reciprocal learning.

Organizations have put together facilitated mentoring specific to minorities, however, to ensure that organizations move from an exclusive hierarchy to a more open and equitable one. Members of minority groups often do not have the same advantage as white males to find mentors to take them under their wing due not to discrimination but to existence of old boys' networks within some organizations. In other organizations, there is concern by those who might otherwise assume mentoring relationships that cultural differences may be too wide to offer the support minority employees and managers need to advance in their careers. In *HR Magazine,* Patricia Digh, a business writer/analyst, writes: "Talented women and minority employees sometimes lack the informal networks and savvy that win promotions for their white male colleagues. Mentoring plans may boost recruitment and retention of high-potential employees—of all kinds."

Structured cross-cultural mentoring is a reaction to today's diverse workplace. Generally, mentors of one ethnic background advise protégés of another culture or background. Without corporate encouragement, mentors have been found to mentor someone who is "like them." They often don't think about reaching out to those who are different in race and culture, let alone gender, because they are either unaware of the need or they fear the unknown. This reality has prompted organizations to move to formal programs. To expect that executives and managers might choose from potential mentees from other cultures has proven unrealistic. But even organizations with structured mentoring initiatives have experienced problems.

To meet diversity goals at Royal Bank, a pilot mentoring process was launched in 1997 and expanded nationally in 1999 using technology to make the process accessible to all employees in any location. Through telephone keypad access, mentors are able to register on a system the skills they will volunteer to develop with a partner, while the partner registers on the system, indicating the skills they want to develop. The skills identified by the partner are those he or she feels are important either to meet the needs of the business unit the individual is in or to increase his or her skills to compete for future positions of interest.

The organization matches mentors and mentees.

Should your organization want to move in this direction, then it should be clear about what it hopes to accomplish from the experience and also what the mentors may expect from the experience.

Among the issues to consider:

- *Awareness of differences.* In a cross-cultural mentoring relationship, it is important to understand how different the partners' assumptions may be about each other. Indeed, schooling the mentoring partners in basic communication skills—those of listening, empathy, and sensitivity in inquiring about culturing differences—along with orientation into different cultural, racial, or gender-based assumptions may be needed.

- *Defined program goals.* Both strategy and goals should be closely aligned and designed to support the business objectives of the organization. For instance, a diversity-driven mentoring program may assist an organization in achieving its strategic goal of increasing the number of minorities in management and leadership ranks for further upward mobility. Or the program may help to meet the goal of retaining minority employees.

- *Involvement of top leadership.* Senior management must champion such programs. The program has to be at the forefront of the organization and communication of senior management's personal commitment must be ongoing. Needless to say, members of top management should participate, setting the tone for employee development, inclusion, and empowerment in the organization.

- *Solicitation of input from participants.* One of the most important tasks for creating an effective diversity-driven mentoring program is to ask potential participants for their input. Individuals who have some degree of influence in shaping the program and have a choice in determining their mentoring partner not only will be of great help in planning but also will be enthusiastic and potentially successful participants in the program.

Making a Group Mentoring Relationship Work

If you are thinking of encouraging a peer or team mentoring group, you need to ask yourself the following questions:

1. Does my organization have the kind of culture to make this effort work?
2. What do I expect my organization to reap from the group experience?
3. What should be the benefit to those who participate in the program?
4. If I had to identify three accomplishments to justify any costs associated with such a program, what would those be? (Be as specific as possible.)
5. What obstacles would be in the way of the mentoring group's effectiveness?
6. Whom, if anyone, should I ask to lead the initial effort? What kind of training would that individual require prior to instituting the program?
7. What would be expected of the group members?
8. How would the organization monitor the effectiveness of the group?
9. What milestones would we set, and what would they represent, in evaluating the effort's success?
10. Assuming that the program is successful, what would be the next step?

Case Study

PEER MENTORING AT OHIO STATE UNIVERSITY

Because coworkers may have had to pull their weight if they weren't doing their job, employees at Ohio State University Extension set up a peer mentoring program with the support of the 88-county University Extension organization. The intent was to shorten the learning curve.

The program begins with a form that each potential mentor and mentee are asked to complete. The bio-sketch form includes information about background, job experience, work-related interests, specialization, hobbies, and so forth. After three months and then 12 months, evaluations are conducted to assess the pairing and the process. Pairs are expected to meet six or more times over a 12-month period.

A special feature of the program is the establishment of a district mentoring contact. A district is defined as an administrative group of 6 to 19 extension units, and a contact in each district helps to locally facilitate and monitor the progress of each mentor-protégé pair. Contacts are responsible for maintaining communication with the pairs, following up with mentees two weeks and three months after pairing, and serving on the Ohio State University mentoring development committee.

Since the peer mentoring program was formed in 1997, over 100 mentor-protégé partnerships have been formed. Although the program was designed to provide support for new employees during their first year, pairings have continued beyond that point. For the experienced mentors, the program has meant considerable improvement in their coaching skills. For new staff, the experience offers temporary support until they become more familiar with other coworkers and find links to others within the organization, sometimes to choose mentors within the organization.

Why is peer mentoring worthy of consideration? Think of the benefits.

- Employees are available to answer questions about day-to-day operational issues.
- New hires feel more at home in the organization in a shorter period of time.
- The initial confusion and uncertainty faced by all new hires is lessened.
- Manager/supervisor time with new employees is freed up to deal with other issues.
- A new hire is able to add value to the workforce more quickly, leading to increased self-confidence.
- The mentor feels more involved and committed to the organization's goals.

Share the message!

Bulk discounts
Discounts start at only 10 copies and range from 30% to 55% off retail price based on quantity.

Custom publishing
Private label a cover with your organization's name and logo. Or, tailor information to your needs with a custom pamphlet that highlights specific chapters.

Ancillaries
Workshop outlines, videos, and other products are available on select titles.

Dynamic speakers
Engaging authors are available to share their expertise and insight at your event.

**Call Dearborn Trade Special Sales at
1-800-621-9621, ext. 4444,
or e-mail trade@dearborn.com**

Dearborn™
Trade Publishing
A **Kaplan Professional** Company